HOW TO START A YOUTUBE CHANNEL FOR FUN & PROFIT

2021 EDITION

The Ultimate Guide to Filming, Uploading & Making Money from Your Videos

By Ann Eckhart

TABLE OF CONTENTS

INTRODUCTION

In 2005, I started a home-based gift basket business, which soon transitioned into an online gift shop selling ceramics, books, and plush. For years, I sold new gift items successfully on both Ebay and Amazon. Unfortunately, as more retailers, and even the wholesale companies that I ordered products from, started selling online directly to customers, I found myself squeezed out of the gift trade.

Fortunately, I had done some "picking" here and there over the years at garage sales, antique malls, and flea markets and was somewhat familiar with the secondhand market. I began turning my focus away from new items to vintage treasures, quickly becoming a regular at local estate sales. And while I was thankful I had another source of sellable goods to fall back on, I knew that I needed to educate myself more on what items to look for that sold well on Ebay; and that is how I found YouTube!

I initially turned to YouTube in search of videos from people who, like me, sold on Ebay as their full-time job. I quickly discovered a YouTube "picking community" (now called the "reselling community") full of people who bought items at garage sales and thrift stores to resell on Ebay. These fellow resellers offered me a vast wealth of information as I transitioned out of selling new gift items and began focusing solely on secondhand treasures.

I began interacting with a small group of YouTuber resellers, commenting on their videos, and offering them whatever advice I could to help them with their own Ebay businesses. After a few months, I finally got the courage to jump into YouTube with my own videos, showing items that I had picked up at estate sales to resell. I shot the videos on my iPhone, and I was able to upload them to YouTube relatively easily. The more videos I shared, the more subscribers my channel received. I was having a lot of fun making videos and interacting with fellow Ebay sellers, so I did not even notice that I was missing out on another benefit of YouTube: making money!

I started my first YouTube channel without even considering the possibility that I could earn money from my videos. Because I did not do my research beforehand, I did not know that I had not set up my channel to properly connect with AdSense, which is the Google advertising platform for YouTube. So, while I continued to post videos and gain subscribers on my channel, I could not earn a penny for my time and effort.

It was not until I started my blog, first called *SeeAnnSave* (which focused on couponing, saving money, and scoring free samples) but now at www.AnnEckhart.com (my homepage for everything that I do), that I figured out my mistake. While setting up my blog and going through the AdSense process to monetize it, I got a notice that I could also create a YouTube channel, connect it with my new AdSense account, and earn money from both my blog AND my videos.

Wait a second, I thought; I already had a YouTube channel. Why can't THAT channel earn me money? It turns out I had not signed up with Google for my first channel, so that channel was unable to earn AdSense revenue. I also could not move my existing channel to fall under my new AdSense account. However, the new channel that Google offered me when I signed up for AdSense on my blog was through Google. And therefore, my new channel could be monetized and could make me money.

Confused? Don't worry, so was I! I now had TWO YouTube channels, one with all my content and subscribers, but that was not earning me anything; and a new channel that had no videos or subscribers, but that had the potential to bring in some cash.

For a while, I tried keeping both of my channels active. However, I eventually ditched the first channel, which was not making me any money, and focused on my new channel, which was starting to earn me some income. I eventually ended up deactivating my original channel altogether, so it is not even on the YouTube site now. For me, it was pointless to put effort into a channel that was not earning me any money. Plus, my first videos had, in my opinion, been of terrible quality. In the end, it was an easy decision to simply delete my first channel and use the experience I had gained on it to put into my new channel, both to produce better quality content and to bring in revenue.

After I decided to stop posting videos on my first channel but before I deleted it completely, I began the process of trying to direct the subscribers on that channel over to my new channel. Initially, some viewers were upset that my old videos were going away. Still, it ended up working out as I reshot those videos and provided better quality content on my new channel. Not only did the subscribers on my first channel eventually come around to my new channel, but I attracted even more viewers and gained more subscribers.

To encourage people to subscribe to my new YouTube channel, I did giveaways, awarding $10 Amazon gift cards every time I reached a new subscriber goal (250, 500, 750, 1000). Before long, my new channel had far more subscribers than my old channel ever had, I was producing better content, AND I was making money!

A few years back, I started a second (or I guess technically a third) YouTube channel devoted to Walt Disney World vacation vlogs. However, I ended up not producing as many travel vlogs as I had initially envisioned. So, I decided it made more sense to move all videos I made to my main channel; and for a couple of years, that second vacation vlog channel sat stagnantly. My main channel was the focus of all of my content, and 95% of that content was reselling related.

In 2019, I started expanding the content on my main YouTube channel to include lifestyle videos such as shopping hauls and unboxings. However, I realized that while I loved creating that type of non-reselling content, having both reselling AND lifestyle videos AND the Disney World vlogs all on the same channel was simply not working.

Why was having various types of videos on one single channel a problem? One would assume that a YouTube channel works just like a television network channel. For instance, you have NBC in your television line-up but likely do not watch all of the shows on NBC. However, you still keep NBC in your channel line-up and tune into the shows you do want to watch.

Viewers look at channels on YouTube differently than television channels. People subscribe to YouTube channels because they look for ONE specific type of content; basically, they view channels as a television show. Unlike NBC, which can air everything from news and soap operas to comedies and documentaries, viewers expect YouTube channels to stick to one type of programming. Viewers expect that new videos on each channel will, in essence, be a new episode of a show.

I have come to think of my YouTube channel as a show that airs on the YouTube network. YouTube functions the same way that NBC does in that it offers a lot of different programming, i.e. channels. Just as you keep NBC in your television line-up, you keep YouTube in your social media network. Just as you only watch some shows on NBC, you only subscribe to some channels on YouTube. And just as you expect your favorite shows on NBC to stay on topic, you expect that the YouTube channels you subscribe to stick to one main topic, too.

In the case of my two YouTube channels, viewers clearly let me know that they wanted my main channel to focus solely on re-selling content. Since my reselling videos were earning me the most money, I decided to dedicate my first and "main" YouTube channel exclusively to reselling; eventually starting a show there called *The Reselling Report* and renaming the channel *The Reselling Report with Ann Eckhart.*

However, because I had viewers who liked my shopping hauls, unboxing, and travel vlogs; and since I enjoyed filming them, I still wanted to produce that type of lifestyle content. But viewers, regardless of whether they watched me for reselling or non-reselling videos, did not like these different topics showing up next to one another on the same channel. So, I renamed my second channel *Ann Eckhart Vlogs,* and today that is where I up-load my non-reselling related videos.

As you can see, I have toyed with multiple YouTube channels and different content over the years. Today I am happily man-aging my two channels, *The Reselling Report with Ann Eckhart* and *Ann Eckhart Vlogs*, putting in about five to ten hours a week be-tween the two. Combined, both channels provide me with the equivalent of the income I would earn from a very nice part-time job outside of the home. However, I only work a fraction of the hours to make the same amount of money on YouTube that I would if I worked for someone else. And I get to do it all while being my own boss and working from the comfort of my own home!

In this book, I will share with you how to start your very own YouTube channel easily and effectively for both fun AND profit. The fun part should always be your priority when making vid-eos. If you are going to put yourself out there in front of po-tentially millions of strangers, you want to make sure you are doing it because you WANT to, not because you think it will make you rich and famous. The fact of the matter is, while there are some very well-know, wealthy YouTubers, most people making videos are merely earning a little bit of extra money. Unless you get hundreds of thousands of subscribers and tens of millions of views on your videos, you are likely looking at only earning some additional spending money, perhaps eventually building it up to part-time income status the way I have, through Google's AdSense program as well as other money-making opportunities that we will go over in this book. But if your dream is to become a full-time YouTube creator, know that if you work hard enough, you CAN make that happen!

Creating YouTube videos has helped me build my brand as it drives traffic to my blog, my books, my Ebay store, and my social media accounts. I make money on YouTube from AdSense, sponsorships, and affiliate links; and I also get many free products sent to me by companies to review on my channels. Plus, I generate numerous book sales from my YouTube viewers who visit my Amazon Author Page. By consistently working on growing my channel, I now not only have a lot of FUN creating content, but I am also making a PROFIT!

So, if you are ready to dive into creating a YouTube channel of your own for both fun and profit, let's get started!

FUN FACTS

10 Most Subscribed To YouTube Channels in 2020:

1. T-Series with 154 million subscribers
2. PewDiePie with 106 million subscribers
3. Cocomelon Nursery Rhymes with 93.8 million subscribers
4. SET India with 82.9 million subscribers
5. 5-Minute Crafts with 68.4 million subscribers
6. WWE with 66.4 million subscribers
7. Kids Diana Show with 63.6 million subscribers
8. Zee Music Company with 61.9 million subscribers
9. Like Nastya Vlog with 60.7 million subscribers

10. Canal KondZilla with 60.4 million subscribers

CHAPTER ONE:

CREATING YOUR YOUTUBE & ADSENSE ACCOUNTS

YouTube was founded by three PayPal employees: Chad Hurley, Steve Chen, and Jawed Karin. They activated the domain name of YouTube.com on February 14, 2005; and their original concept was that the site would be an online dating series. However, when that idea failed, the young entrepreneurs instead focused on making YouTube a place for non-computer experts to publish, upload, and stream videos through standard web browsers and household modems. Google purchased YouTube in 2006 for $1.65 billion in stock.

Over the years, YouTube has grown from a little niche website to a platform with over two billion users worldwide, with 79% of those users also having their own YouTube accounts. 94% of American users between the ages of 18-44 access YouTube at least once a month, with a billion hours of content consumed worldwide daily. 62% of businesses use YouTube to promote their brands, and 90% of people claim to discover new products via YouTube. Today more than 70% of YouTube watch time comes from mobile devices via the YouTube app. And 400 hours of video are uploaded to YouTube every minute.

Needless to say, YouTube has become a part of everyday life for a large population of people across the globe. With content that includes cooking, crafting, traveling, vlogging, gaming, beauty, style, parenting, news, comedy, and business, there is truly something for everyone to watch on YouTube.

So, you may be wondering if there is a place for you on this over-crowded site? The answer is YES! Anyone can start a YouTube channel today and work to make it successful. The key is that you have to actually start and then be consistent.

YouTube creators can make money on the site because Google owns the actual website itself. Google enabled channels to start making money from their videos in 2008. Not only has this partnership been beneficial for channel creators, but it has also proved to be a lucrative opportunity for advertisers as they can reach customers across the globe for a fraction of the cost of television advertising. YouTube currently runs ads on over a billion video views every week. According to Google:

- 40 million users access the YouTube homepage every day
- Google sells seven different kinds of homepage ads
- Audiences utilize hundreds of millions of searches on YouTube every day
- Promoted videos are the search advertising product that helps drive traffics to individual videos
- Over 2 billion videos are watched every single day on the site

Since Google owns YouTube and controls the AdSense advertising that pays you for your videos, you must first sign up with Google to create a YouTube channel that will earn you ad revenue. As I talked about in the *Introduction* to this book, when I started my first YouTube channel, I did not sign up through Google but instead registered through a different email account. Because I did not sign up for my YouTube channel through a Google email address, my first channel could not be monetized and never earned me any money. So, you MUST register with Google to make money from your YouTube channel!

GOOGLE ACCOUNT: To sign up for a Google account that will allow you to create a YouTube account and channel, head to the Google Account sign-up page at: https://tinyurl.com/y75ms8mr. The registration process is quick, easy, and completely free. You will be able to create a Google account and a YouTube account, a Google email address, and a YouTube channel, all in one place. Simply follow the online prompts to complete the process. Note that having a Google account allows you to create your own YouTube channel and give you your own YouTube account, which will enable you to interact with other creators' content (such as subscribing to channels, giving videos a 'thumbs up,' and leaving comments). Many people who have YouTube accounts never create their own channels; but the option is already built in once you have an account.

CHANNEL NAME: Choose your YouTube channel name wisely. Google usually prompts you to make it your actual name, but you can select any name you like (as long as another account is not currently using it). While you may just be starting on YouTube for fun now, you do not want to limit yourself from growing your brand in the future. There are many established, successful YouTube channels out there with names unrelated to their content because the people behind them never anticipated how large their channels would grow.

I named my first YouTube channel, the one that is no longer active, my Ebay store name, the name that my reselling business was registered under. When I started my blog, I originally called it *SeeAnnSave* as I was posting about couponing and free samples. So, when I started a new YouTube channel under my new Google account, I also named it *SeeAnnSave*. I then worked to 'brand' that name across all my social networking sites (Facebook, Twitter, and Instagram). However, in late 2017 I renamed my blog to just my name, *Ann Eckhart.* I then had to rename my YouTube channel along with all my social media accounts, too. It was a considerable undertaking; so, think long and hard before naming your channel to avoid the headache of changing it later.

Note that your channel name is the same name on your Google account; changing your Google account name will automatically change your YouTube channel name. However, the URL of your channel can only be changed by contacting YouTube directly. My main channel URL still ends with *seeannsave*; and my second channel URL ends with *seeannatwdw* as I initially started it as a Walt Disney World vacation vlog channel. While I changed my Google account names so that my primary channel NAME is now *The Reselling Report with Ann Eckhart,* and my second channel NAME is *Ann Eckhart Vlogs*, the URL's for both channels have not changed. It is confusing, I know! I still have not bothered to contact YouTube to ask about changing my URL's as in the end, the website address itself does not matter too much. It is the name of the channel that I personally feel is important. Most viewers will either search for your channel name or just subscribe to your channel outright to find your videos; very few people will actually type in your channel's URL address, much less even know what it is.

ADSENSE ACCOUNT: While you used to start earning money right out of the gate on YouTube, in 2019, Google changed the requirements for becoming monetized. i.e., allowing you to place ads on your videos to earn a cut of the revenue from them. Now a channel needs to have 1,000 subscribers AND 4,000 hours of views before it can start making AdSense money.

While these new requirements are frustrating for new YouTube creators, you can get your channel to monetization standards rather quickly with dedication and consistency. I will go over ways to grow your channel later in this book.

According to Google, AdSense works in three steps:

1. You make your ad spaces available by pasting ad code on your blog or website, as well as placing ads on your YouTube videos.
2. The highest paying ads appear on your site as advertisers bid to show in your ad spaces in real-time auctions.
3. Creators get paid directly from Google, with Google handling the process of billing all advertisers for the ads that show up on your content.

As part of the AdSense Program, Google delivers ads to your blog/website/YouTube channel via their Google Ads system. Google then pays you for the advertisements displayed based on user clicks on ads OR ad impressions, depending on the ad type.

Creators cannot choose the ads that appear on their sites/videos. Google uses three methods to determine which ads are placed; according to them, these are:

1. **Contextual Targeting:** Google technology uses factors such as keyword analysis, word frequency, font size, and the over link structure of the internet to determine what a site or video is about and precisely how to match Google ads to that particular content.
2. **Placement Targeting:** Under this format, advertisers can choose specific ad placements to run their ads. Ads that are placement-targeted may not be precisely related to a page's content, but are instead hand-selected by advertisers who have decided that there is a match between what your readers/viewers are interested in.
3. **Personalized Targeting:** This offering enables advertisers to reach users based on their interests, demographics, types of websites they visit, the apps on their mobile devices, the cookies on their web browsers, the activity on their devices, previous interactions with other Google ads, and their own Google Account activ-

ity and information.

To monetize your videos, you will first need to become a You-Tube Partner, which we will discuss in the next section of this chapter. However, if you have a blog or website, you will want to go ahead and sign up for a Google AdSense account now as you can start earning money from ads on your site immediately. Simply visit https://www.google.com/adsense/start/ to begin the application process. Note that you will need to go through a verification process to qualify for an account, including providing your social security number for tax purposes and your bank routing information for direct deposit of your earnings.

You can choose to have your AdSense earnings mailed to you or sent via direct deposit to your bank account. You must reach $100 in total AdSense earnings across all platforms (blog/website/YouTube) to receive a payout. Since I have AdSense through both my blog and YouTube, I easily meet that $100 monthly threshold; and the money is automatically deposited into my bank account around the third week of the month. At the end of the year, Google sends me a tax form detailing my earnings, which I then simply give to my accountant so that he can add it to my income tax returns. Yes, you must report your YouTube earnings to the IRS; I will go over this topic more later on in this book.

Once you have completed the application process and have been approved for an AdSense account, you can begin placing AdSense ads on your blog or website. However, you will have to wait to be eligible to join the YouTube Partner Program to start monetizing your videos.

YOUTUBE PARTNERSHIP: After you have created your Google, YouTube, and AdSense accounts, there is one more step you will need to take before you can start earning money on your videos, and that is to become a **YouTube Partner**. Once your channel reaches 1,000 subscribers and 4,000 watch hours, YouTube will prompt you to sign up with their YouTube Partner Program.

According to YouTube, "The YouTube Partner Program (YPP) gives creators greater access to YouTube resources and features," including access to YouTube's creator support teams, copyright match tools, and monetization features.

The minimum eligibility requirements to join the YouTube Partner Program include:

- Following all of the current YouTube monetization policies (these are frequently updated; once you are going through the application process, you will be prompted to agree to them)
- Live in a country or region where the YPP is available
- Have 4,000 valid public watch hours within 12 months
- Have more than 1,000 subscribers
- Have a linked AdSense account (again, this is an excellent reason to create your AdSense account even before you are eligible to apply to be a YouTube Partner as you will be ready to go once you meet the requirements)

Here is an abbreviate YouTube Partner Program application checklist:

1. Make sure your channel follows all policies and guidelines. When you apply, you will go through a standard review process to check if your channel meets these standards.
2. Enable 2-Step Verification for your Google account, which means you will protect your account with both your password and an additional device.
3. Have at least 1,000 subscribers and 4,000 valid watch hours on your channel.
4. Sign TPP terms to be notified when you are eligible to apply to become a YouTube Partner. You can do this

manually, although YouTube will prompt you once you meet the subscriber and view thresholds.

5. Make sure you only have ONE AdSense account (you cannot have multiple accounts under your name)

6. Once you sign the YouTube Partner Program terms and connect your AdSense account, your channel will be put into a queue for review. Both automated systems and human reviewers will then review your channel's content before being accepted into the YouTube Partner Program. Note that it can take up to a month for your account to be reviewed; it depends on how many other accounts are in line before you and how much staff is currently available to conduct reviews.

MONETIZE YOUR VIDEOS: Your videos must be monetized for them to start earning income. Monetization means you are authorizing YouTube to place ads in your videos and that you agree that no copyrighted materials (music and video clips from TV shows, movies, or other licensed sources) appear in your footage.

Having an AdSense account does not automatically mean your videos will earn money; you need to manually monetize each of your videos. This is done in the **YouTube Studio** section of your YouTube account. Simply click on a video, choose the **edit icon** (it looks like a pencil), and then click on the "$" icon on the left-hand side of the page.

You will be brought to the **Video Monetization** page of the video you choose. Select **On** from the Monetization drop-down menu. A pop-up box will appear on your screen titled **Tell us what's in your video**. Here you will need to confirm whether your video contains **Inappropriate language, Adult content, Violence, Shocking content, Harmful or dangerous acts, Drug-related content, Hateful Content, Firearms-related content,** and/or **Sensitive issues.** YouTube strictly controls videos that contain any of those types of content, so unless your videos contain any of them, you will simply check **None of the above** before hitting the **Submit** button.

You will then be taken back to the **Video monetization** page. Here you will want to check every box under the **Type of ads** section: **Display ads, Overlay ads, Sponsored cards, Skippable video ads,** and **Non-skippable video ads.** You will also want to check every box under **Location of video ads: Before video (pre-roll), During video (mid-roll),** and **After video (post-roll).** Click **Save** to finalize these options.

If your video is over ten minutes long, you will also want to click on the **MANAGE MID-ROLL** option found under **During video (mid-roll).** The advertisements that run in the middle of videos typically bring in the most revenue; so, you will want to make sure they are placed effectively in your videos. YouTube will automatically place them for you if you wish, but I personally like to make my own selections to ensure that the ads are not too close together. Sometimes YouTube will put in way too many ads, which will turn viewers off, or they may not put enough in. They also tend to stick them in strange places, such as at the very end of the video.

I typically place my ads every four to six minutes depending on how long the video is. For instance, I will place ads for a fifteen-minute video at four, eight, and twelve minutes. Placing ad breaks is easy; I simply **click on the "+" next to AD BREAK** and click to add as many individual placements as I want. Then, under the **PLACE AUTOMATICALLY** column, I enter in the time stamp for each. You can easily change these, so do not worry about making a mistake. You can also manually move each ad break at the bottom of the page. I will walk you through the step-by-step process I go through to monetize my videos later on in this book.

Once you have your ad breaks where you want them, simply click on the **CONTINUE** button to confirm your selection. You will be brought back to the **Video monetization** page, but you are now done placing the ads on that video,

Make sure to go back into your old videos, the ones that were not monetized initially, to monetize them, too. The mid-roll ads are incredibly important, so even though it can be time-consuming to update your older videos with them, it will be worth it in terms of your earnings. Note that I will be going into more detail about how to upload, edit, and prepare your videos in "Chapter Seven: A Day in The Life."

I know that the steps to set up and monetize your YouTube channel can seem overwhelming. Signing up for a Google account, an AdSense account, and a YouTube account, plus then applying for the YouTube Partner Program, all take time. And you need to make sure that the information you provide is accurate; after all, you are asking that Google pay you for ads that are placed in and on your content. It's almost like applying for a job. So, be patient and make sure to follow all the instructions when you are filling out your applications. However, you only have to do these things once. After you have all your accounts set up and can monetize your YouTube videos, you will be able to relax and enjoy the monthly deposits of money into your bank account!

FUN FACTS

The First Youtube Channels To Launch On The Site In 2005:

- Brats and Bereta (sketch comedy)
- Rebecca Black (singer)
- Brookers (comedy)
- Iman Crosson (comedy)
- Darude (music)
- Lisa Donovan (entertainment)
- How It Should Have Ended (web series)
- Smosh (sketch comedy)
- Venus Records & Tapes (India)
- Cory Williams (entertainment)

- The Young Turks (news)

CHAPTER TWO:

FILMING EQUIPMENT & SET-UP

My guess is that you are eager to read this section of the book because you want me to tell you exactly which camera you need to purchase to film your videos and what computer you need to edit them on, right? Well, because there are so many ways to upload and edit videos, and because new cameras and equipment are continually being released, you will need to do your research to find out what, if any, items you need to purchase to start a YouTube channel. You may find that you already own the tools you need.

You can actually film, edit, and upload YouTube videos using just an iPhone; in fact, I have only ever produced my YouTube videos using an iPhone. I use apps to edit and upload my videos, and I use a basic laptop for completing the back-end production aspects for my channel. In Chapter Seven of this book, "A Day In The Life," I will go over the step-by-step process for using an iPhone to film videos.

The necessary equipment you will need to run a YouTube channel are:

CAMERA: Either an iPhone or a DSLR camera work best for filming YouTube videos. Many successful YouTube creators offer videos explaining their filming process along with the cameras they use. The best advice I can give you is to search YouTube for "best camera to film YouTube videos" to see what comes up. Look for the most recent videos as those will give you information on the latest models. DSLR cameras range from $100 to well over $1,000.

As a basic guideline, you want a camera that can film in HD, whether 720p or 1080p. HD (high-definition) is the highest quality filming available for personal cameras and results in video footage that appears super crisp and clear. Most phones even film in HD these days, including the iPhone that I use. While I upload from my iPhone directly to YouTube, you will need to transfer your video footage to your computer via the camera's SD memory card if you use a stand-alone camera.

At the end of this chapter, I give you a list of the current top ten cameras for filming YouTube videos. Note, however, that these are the best and most expensive options available; there are many lower-priced models that work just as well, especially when you are just starting your channel.

LIGHTING EQUIPMENT: If you intend to film vlog-style videos, i.e., footage of you as you go about your everyday life, then you will not have to worry about purchasing lighting equipment as you'll be using whatever light happens to be available in the setting you are filming in, including natural light. However, if you plan to mainly film sit-down videos where you are just sitting in front of a camera, you may want to look into purchasing a studio 40W ring light lamp. However, before investing in a ring light, test out filming videos in natural life, either outside or sitting by a large window. Save buying a ring light for when your channel is established, and you intend to grow it.

VIDEO EDITING SOFTWARE: I use the free iMovie app on my iPhone to edit my YouTube videos; Apple's iMovie is also available for Mac computers. iMovie is the most popular of all the video editing software as it is easy to use and comes with most Mac computer systems. If you do not have a Mac computer, you will need to look into other software, such as Shortcut, Adobe Premiere, Lightworks, Final Cut Pro, or Corel. Just as I advised that you search YouTube for the latest camera reviews, I suggest you do the same for video editing software as new options are continually being released; and what software you need depends on the computer system you are using. However, if you plan to start your channel by filming on an iPhone, you will be fine just using the iMovie app from Apple's App Store.

COMPUTER: While I do the bulk of my YouTube work on my iPhone, I still utilize my laptop for my videos. I find it much easier to type in my titles and description box information using my computer versus my small phone keyboard. I also like accessing the YouTube Studio feature from my desktop to adjust my video specifics and monetization setting. Fortunately, YouTube studio works with both Mac and PCs; so, the computer you use for editing videos will work just fine for any other YouTube work you do. Note that while most large YouTube channels rely on Mac computers to edit, there are options for PC users, as well. As always, try to start your channel using the equipment you already own as you can always upgrade later on.

TRIPOD: I wish I could tell you the very best tripod to purchase for filming YouTube videos, one that will hold your camera steady while you film. But the truth is that I myself do not use a tripod. If I am filming a sit-down video, I just prop my iPhone up on some books or boxes. And when I am vlogging, I use a handheld tripod that offers me a better grip for on-the-go filming, and that can also sit on a tabletop if I want to put it down for a moment. However, just like with cameras and software, a quick search of "best tripods for filming YouTube videos" will yield you results that match the camera you intend to film with. Most YouTube creators who film sit-down videos do use a tripod and a light system such as these models on Amazon: https:// amzn.to/342RbxT .

Some other tips to consider when you are filming YouTube videos are:

QUALITY: No matter what equipment you end up using to film, edit, and upload your YouTube videos, quality is vital. Even though I film on my iPhone, I still upload my videos in High Definition. I make sure that I hold the camera steady while filming and that I have plenty of light. I also hold the camera horizontally as filming vertically creates a black bar on either side of the video.

I have seen so many horrible YouTube videos where the footage is dark, the volume is on mute, and the screen is jerky. I have even seen videos that were upside down! Before you make your videos live, preview them first. While they do not have to be up to the Hollywood standard of film quality, you want them to be as clear and steady as possible. If a video looks terrible to you when you are previewing it, imagine what viewers will think when you upload it.

Redo videos that are not of good quality. Practice makes perfect! I have refilmed many videos during my time on YouTube. I would rather take the time to completely refilm a video than have a poor-quality clip be viewed by thousands and potentially millions of people.

SPEAK UP: A big problem I see with many new YouTube creators is that their videos' volume is so low that I cannot even hear what they say. When filming, make sure you are speaking in a clear, loud voice. While you do not want to scream at your viewers, you do want to make sure they can hear what you are saying. Ensure there is no background noise while you are filming, such as music or the television. Turn your phone to silent and film in a quiet room with the door closed. If you are vlogging, make sure that your hand does not inadvertently cover up the microphone. Also, be aware that most music is copyrighted, meaning you will not be able to monetize videos where background music is being played, such as in stores. The hardest part of vlogging is making sure no copyrighted music is picked up by the microphone. Nothing is worse than taking the time to vlog only to have YouTube put a copyright strike on the video due to music in the background.

BACKGROUNDS: You have likely seen YouTube videos with professionally designed backgrounds, as well as those shot in what looks to be the home of a hoarder. While you do not need to spend thousands of dollars to make the background of your videos look like it came straight from a home decor magazine, you do want to make sure to film in a clean, clutter-free space with a simple backdrop.

For sit-down videos, I have a dedicated space in my office where I film. I have bookshelves behind me; I change out the décor on the shelves seasonally. In the past, I will admit that my backgrounds were not as nice as I would have liked them to be, especially ones where there were piles of Ebay inventory behind me (although, in my defense, I was filming videos about Ebay!). I am always trying to improve the quality of my videos, including my backgrounds. Note that if you are vlogging, you do not have to worry about creating a pretty backdrop as you'll be filming yourself in whatever place you happen to be. However, you still want to be aware of your surroundings so that viewers are focused on you, not on what might be going on in the shot behind you.

One of my favorite backgrounds that I see many female YouTubers use is to film with their bed behind them, and twinkle lights (the kind you put on Christmas trees) strung up around the bed frame or window. This lighting arrangement creates such a lovely scene for filming. Other people film with the nicest part of their kitchen or living room behind them. Gamers and review channels often have bookshelves behind them full of neatly arranged products. You want your background to align with your content. For instance, if you film cooking videos, you will want to use your kitchen as your backdrop, not your dirty garage.

Suppose you are serious about making YouTube an actual business that earns you a decent income. In that case, you will want to consider dedicating a space for filming that is well lit and nicely decorated. However, if you are just starting out or you are only interested in making a bit of money from YouTube, do the best with what you have. Some of the biggest YouTube channels on the site today got their start with the creators filming while sitting on the floor of their bedrooms or even sitting in their cars with the cameras propped up on their steering wheels!

CAMERA ANGLE: Finding the angle from which you look your best on camera can be a challenge. Most of us feel we have a "good side," the side of our face from which we look a bit more attractive than the other. However, video is much different from still photography in that you move around on film and are not sitting in a stationary position. Therefore, it is more important to have the camera facing you directly and slightly above you. Having to look up a bit to the camera helps eliminate the double chin phenomenon!

As with background, the camera angle is something I have always been challenged by. While I do have an iPhone tripod, it is a flimsy thing that does not hold my iPhone very well. So, for sit-down videos, I just prop my iPhone up on some books or boxes. When vlogging, I now have a portable tripod that I can attach to my phone that also converts to a stand; I can just prop the stand up on a flat surface to film when I am on the go. And the handle helps me hold the camera steady when I am vlogging.

Of course, if you choose not to appear on screen, you need not focus on how you look but instead on how what you are filming looks like, whether it is a single stationary item or a moving scene. If you are filming cooking videos, for instance, you will want a tripod that holds the camera to look over what you are preparing. Or perhaps you can have someone else hold the camera and film you. Do not be surprised if your first videos do not look that great as it takes time to learn how to film best. Try different angles and methods until you find what you are most comfortable with.

KEEP IT CLASSY: While you do not have to have your hair and make-up professionally done every time you film a YouTube video, you do want to take care of your appearance. Looking as clean and neat as possible goes a long way towards presenting yourself in the best possible light, even if you are simply wearing basic jeans and a tee-shirt. If you smoke, do not smoke on camera. Avoid chewing gum while filming. Be aware of your language; swearing not only turns off viewers, but it can result in YouTube demonetizing your video. And do your best to clean up your surrounding area. No one wants to see your overflowing trash can or a pile of dirty laundry in the background of your videos.

FUN FACTS

Current Top-Rated Cameras For Filming YouTube Videos:

- Canon PowerShot G7 X Mark III
- Sony RX100 Mark VII
- DJI Osmo Pocket
- GoPro Hero9 Black
- DJI Osmo Action
- Canon EOS M6 Mark II
- Sony A6600
- Panasonic GH5
- Sigma fp
- Huawei P30 Pro

CHAPTER THREE:

YOUR CHANNEL'S THEME
& CONTENT

My first YouTube channel was dedicated solely to my reselling business on Ebay, showing viewers the items I sourced at estate sales and thrift stores to sell online along with all my tips and tricks for how to make money on the site. I did not really talk about anything else but Ebay on that channel, and the people who subscribed to me were there to learn and/or talk about just Ebay, too. I did not do videos to make money (and I did not make any on my first channel); I simply enjoyed sharing my knowledge about reselling with others and connecting with other people who did the same. As I have talked about already, I did, however, jump at the chance to monetize my content by starting a new channel through Google. Still, even on my second (now primary) YouTube channel, my content was strictly about reselling

However, over the years, I started experimenting with different content on different channels. Personally, I have found it better to separate my lifestyle videos from my reselling videos, having them each on their own dedicated channels. Starting out, though, I would recommend you start with just ONE YouTube channel. You want to master running a single channel before you ever even think about having two or more. And most You-

Tube creators only have one channel. If I were only making videos about Ebay, I would only have one channel; reselling is such a small niche that it really does well with a dedicated channel, meaning its best for me to put other content on a separate channel. But if the videos you intend to share all fall under the same general theme, such as lifestyle or gaming, then you will be just fine with all your content on one channel.

As I have already discussed earlier in this book, I went into YouTube thinking that having a channel was like having your own television network. Unfortunately, that is not the way viewers see it. While you have NBC in your television channel line-up, it is likely that you only watch a few of their shows on their network. However, you do not take NBC out of your TV package just because you do not watch every show they air. You watch the shows you want to and simply ignore the rest.

YouTube, however, is different. Viewers look at the entire YouTube site as if it were a television network with the individual channels functioning as separate shows. You have YouTube on your smartphone or computer, and you watch the shows, i.e., the channels you like. However, you do not watch ALL the channels because you are not interested in all the different "shows." But you keep YouTube installed on your devices the same way you keep the various networks, such as NBC, installed on your television lineup.

Think of it like this: Say your favorite television show is *Friends*. *Friends* originally aired on the NBC television network, but it is now shown on many other channels, and even streaming services, via syndication. Imagine if you were happily watching an episode of *Friends*, but then the following show to air was *Law & Order*. Now, you may actually like *Law & Order*, but for this example, let's say that you don't. If you were watching *Friends* on your television or streaming service and *Law & Order* came on, you would just change the channel to a different show.

However, what if *Friends* had its very own dedicated television channel. You would need to subscribe to this channel separate from your other television channels. But since *Friends* is your absolute favorite show, you are thrilled to be able to subscribe to a channel that is dedicated only to *Friends*. However, imagine one day that when you went to watch *Friends* on this dedicated channel, suddenly they also started showing episodes of *Law & Order*. Now this unique channel that you subscribed just to watch *Friends* is showing you a completely different show, making it hard for you even to find the episodes of *Friends* that you want to watch. Would you stay subscribed to the channel or look for better content elsewhere? If this select *Friends* channel were a YouTube channel, most YouTube subscribers would unsubscribe once other shows was introduced.

Some YouTube viewers will subscribe and stay subscribed to channels because they like all or at least most of the "shows" (individual videos) they are seeing. However, if they start to dislike more "shows" (individual videos) than they actually like, they may unsubscribe from that channel. The most loyal of my YouTube viewers watch the majority of videos I put out depending on which channel they are subscribed to. Some viewers watch all the videos on both of my channels, while others only watch one channel. And still, others only check in periodically depending on the video topic. Trying to mix vacation vlogs in with reselling videos was a disaster for me as it confused my viewers as to what my channel (i.e., the show) was about, and I lost subscribers on both channels.

No matter what topic I am filming a video about or how much engagement I am getting between my channels, I try only to make videos that I WANT to make, ones that are FUN and INTERESTING to me. Even though I am now earning money on YouTube, the main reason I make videos is for my own personal enjoyment. YouTube has improved my public speaking skills and increased my confidence. It has allowed me to network and make new friends with people I would have never met otherwise. And it has also helped me grow my book sales and make money from sponsorships. I make YouTube videos for FUN, and as a bonus, I also earn a PROFIT.

While I have covered a wide variety of topics in my years on YouTube, you will likely be looking to only film videos on one subject. Do not follow the trends to go with what is popular. Make videos about what you LOVE and the subscribers, and Ad-Sense revenue will follow.

Some common YouTube channel themes and video topics are:

Cooking & Baking: Do you love to cook up new recipes and share your favorite baking recipes with friends? If you love to be in the kitchen, you can share your culinary knowledge via YouTube videos. You do not have to be an expert chef, either; even the most straightforward recipes are popular on YouTube. I have posted several cooking and baking videos over the years; all my recipes are super easy to make but get many views. Most of these videos are relatively short in length, but they are some of my top-earning AdSense videos!

Crafting: There is a vast crafting community on YouTube, so if you are a crafter, you will find others who share your passion. Whether you want to film tutorials or simply show off your craft supply hauls and projects, you will find an eager audience awaiting your content. Beading, scrapbooking, knitting, quilting, card making, and any other type of craft can make great videos, whether they are tutorials or hauls. The crafting community on YouTube is huge, so be sure to connect with other crafters who are making videos by liking and commenting on their videos, too. I am not a crafter myself, but I have done well with some DIY Dollar Tree tutorials.

Diet & Fitness: Another hot YouTube channel theme is diet and fitness. Whether it is nutrition or weight loss, bodybuilding, or running, many people turn to YouTube to get in shape. Natural food and specialty diets (gluten-free, vegan, raw) are also popular video topics.

Gaming: Video game channels are among the most popular on YouTube, with the top creators earning millions of dollars a year. If you love to play video games, you can turn your hobby into income on YouTube.

Gardening: If you have a green thumb, consider sharing your gardening skills on YouTube. Many people want to learn about plants, flowers, and vegetable gardening. Share all your gardening information and watch your subscriber list (and AdSense money) grow along with your plants!

Hauls: Love to shop? Share your shopping hauls with your You-Tube subscribers. Even a trip to the grocery store to stock the fridge can make for an exciting video. Trader Joe's and Costco hauls are wildly popular. I film quite a few haul videos on my personal YouTube channel from stores such as Dollar Tree, Bath & Body Works, and Target, and they are always a big hit. Sometimes I even film "shop with me" videos and take my viewers along with me in vlog-style videos.

How-To: As I talked about in the filming equipment section, there are thousands of how-to videos on YouTube that cover nearly every topic you can think of, including how to film and edit YouTube videos. If there is an area or areas you are proficient in (computers, carpentry, crafting), creating how-to videos can be a great source of videos for your channel. Some channels are entirely dedicated to showing how to put together items purchased online. I have recently relied on YouTube videos to show me how to build a shelf and also to assemble a pressure washer, both of which I ordered on Amazon. Creators of these videos not only make money via AdSense but also from the affiliate links they provide. For instance, in the video I watched on the pressure washer, the creator linked the pressure washer in the video's description box. The creator then earned an Amazon commission from anyone who clicked on the link and made a purchase on the site.

Make-up & Fashion: Beauty bloggers and vloggers are all over YouTube, and they are some of the most successful channels on the site. Most YouTube "beauty gurus" have an accompanying blog to support their videos and earn more ad revenue. If you love make-up, skincare, and/or clothing, sharing your personal style tips with others may be the perfect theme for your channel.

In addition to doing make-up tutorials, beauty gurus also do first impression reviews of products, shopping hauls (from stores such as ULTA, Sephora, and Bath & Body Works), make-up storage, make-up collections, nail polish collections, closet organization, jewelry collections, and clothing hauls. The beauty category is very crowded on YouTube. Only start a beauty channel because you LOVE make-up and clothes; if you are good at applying makeup and have a style that impresses others, the subscribers and ad revenue will follow.

Mommy Videos: Are you a mom-to-be, or do you already have little ones in the home? There are many other mothers out there who you can connect with, whether by merely sharing your baby's milestones or talking about what you feed your toddler. There are many women (and men!) out there who love to interact with other parents. Homeschooling videos are also popular, as are reviews of baby and children products. Other videos that typically receive many views are kids' clothing hauls, back-to-school hauls and tips, and what presents you buy your kids for the holidays.

Organization: Organizing is another hot YouTube channel theme. How to organize your house, office, car, kid's toys, crafts, garage, and basement can all make for great videos. If you excel at organizing, you may think there is no audience for this topic, but believe me that there are people out there who would love to watch you organize something as simple as a junk drawer! Organizing your home on a budget from dollar stores is something many people produce videos on, too.

Picking/Reselling: I got started on YouTube by interacting with the "picking community" (now called the "reselling community"), which is a group of people who buy items from garage sales and thrift stores to resell on Ebay, Etsy, Poshmark, Amazon, or in antique mall booths. Many people would love to see your finds and hear about your sales if you are a reseller. Sharing your tips about reselling both online and off will gain you an audience.

Reviews: Do you love to read or go to the movies? Are friends always asking you to recommend your favorite video games or CDs? Do you always buy the latest gadgets? Millions of people turn to YouTube for reviews, so if you love books, movies, television, video games, music, and/or electronics, consider making a channel where you offer your opinions! If you review products, you will likely start to be contacted by companies offering to send you free items in exchange for video reviews. In just the past few months alone, I have been sent a robotic vacuum, an air fryer, and a humidifier, all for free just for showing them on my YouTube channel.

If you do plan to do reviews, note that copyright issues will prevent you from using clips of movies, video games, television shows, or music; but you can hold up your own copy of a DVD or CD if you want some sort of visual. Another way to make money on reviews is to sign up for an Amazon Associates account and put your referral link in the description bar to the item you are reviewing. If someone buys something through your link, whether it was the item you reviewed or something else, you will earn a commission on their purchase. I will talk more about the Amazon Associates program later in this book.

Tags: Tags are trendy amongst YouTubers. Tags are simply question and answer lists, such as "50 Random Facts About Me". There are tags galore on YouTube, and they give you an easy way to create content as all you must do is answer the questions. The last chapter in this book is filled with all sorts of tags you can film. Tags are especially helpful if you are just starting out and unsure of what kinds of videos you want to make.

Travel: Do you love to travel? Perhaps you take frequent road trips or cruises, or maybe you are an RV or camping enthusiast. There are lots of YouTube viewers who would love to see your travel footage, including your packing tips, dining recommendations, and money-saving advice. I have filmed many Walt Disney Vacation vlogs for my YouTube channel over the years.

Vlogging: People worldwide chronicle their lives through vlogs, many doing so every day. Note that vlogging is very time consuming and can feel like an invasion of privacy if you are not careful; however, lots of folks are earning a part-time and even full-time income on YouTube by sharing 10 to 20-minute snippets of their daily lives. Note that you do not have to be a daily vlogger to have a vlog channel; you can film as many or as few vlogs as you would like, although it helps stick to a schedule, such as posting vlogs three times a week.

Suppose you enjoy vlogging but don't want to commit to a set vlogging schedule. In that case, you can simply vlog whenever you are doing something particularly exciting or during a "vlogging month" such as "Vlogmas" (vlogging for Christmas), "Vlogtober" (vlogging every day in October), "VEDA" (vlogging every day in April), or "Vlogust" (vlogging every day in August). I, myself, have done "Vlogust," "Vlogtober," and "Vlogmast" in the past.

The hard part about vlogging for me has been that the subscribers who love vlogs REALLY love vlogs and desperately want them to continue daily. It is a lot of pressure to keep up with daily uploads. For me, another downside to vlogging is that you are exposing yourself to more criticism and scrutiny than a regular sit-down or one-topic video might bring. Even when you only show 10-minutes out of a 24-hour day, viewers start to assume that they know everything about you and can either be overly friendly (i.e., a bit like a stalker!) or too critical.

Most daily vloggers start out interacting with viewers in the comments but stop doing so as their subscribers increase because they feel the need to guard their privacy more closely. If vlogging interests you, consider starting off by doing it once a week. You can always expand to more frequent vlogs if you decide you really enjoy doing them and do not feel like you are exposing too much of your personal life.

FUN FACTS

Top 10 Current Youtube Channel Themes:

1. Unboxing videos (opening products, subscription boxes, and devices)
2. Reviewing gadgets (incredibly lucrative if you review products that you have an affiliate link for so that you can earn not only AdSense but also affiliate income)
3. Reaction videos (reacting to popular videos, TV shows, music, and films)
4. Gaming videos (streaming a gaming session)
5. Daily hack videos (tips and tricks for everyday life)
6. Prank videos (recording reactions from playing pranks on people)
7. Fitness and health videos (exercise and weight-loss)
8. Cooking videos (baking, instapot, and slow cooker recipes, and special diets such as Keto)
9. Make-up tutorial videos (how-to's and reviews)
10. Animated videos (videography and animation)
11. Animal and pet videos (vlogs with your pets, care how-to's, and product reviews)

CHAPTER FOUR:

HOW TO EARN MONEY ON YOUTUBE

So far, in this book, I have already discussed how you make money on YouTube via AdSense; but there are other ways you can bring in even more income with your videos. While AdSense will be your first money-making stream, it will likely not be your last as you grow your channel.

ADSENSE: In the first chapter of this book, I covered the basics of monetizing your videos with AdSense as part of the YouTube Partner program. But you must understand how AdSense works and how you can best utilize it on your channel.

AdSense is the route in which Google sells advertising. You have likely seen Google-branded pop-up ads on various websites; those ads' money is processed through AdSense. When you are monetized on YouTube, Google will run ads on your videos; just like ads that appear on text-based websites, the ads that appear on videos are purchased and sold through AdSense. Google Ads and AdSense are nearly the same.

Whether on a website or in a YouTube video, the ads that are shown to you have been matched to the content you are either reading or watching. The ads are created and paid for by advertising companies. These companies pay Google to run the ads, and Google splits the money with the content creators, both on blogs and websites and YouTube.

How much you will earn via Google AdSense depends on several different factors such as the type of ads placed on your videos, how viewers respond to the ads, and the cost that each particular advertiser is paying Google to run their ads. The more a brand pays for an ad, the more you will make it if people watch your video.

On YouTube, how much money a video makes is first determined by the **CPM**. CPM stands for "cost per 1,000 impressions", and the CPM is what YouTube is able to charge advertisers for videos placed on your ads. While you are not paid the CPM, it is an important factor in determining your **RPM**, which is your cut of the revenue.

CPM's can be as low as $1 and as high as hundreds of dollars; it all depends on the video's content. Again, this is the amount that YouTube is charging advertisers, not the amount you are paid. Your RPM is usually half of your CPM, so a high CPM typically results in a high RPM.

As a YouTube creator, you are paid per 1,000 views on all your videos combined throughout the month. As an example, my general lifestyle videos earn around $12 CPM per 1,000 views. However, my reselling videos earn, on average, $35 CPM per 1,000 views. Why the difference? Well, lifestyle videos are a dime a dozen on YouTube; there is so much competition in this category that content creators end up splitting the share of advertising between thousands of different channels. However, reselling is a tiny, niche category, but one with a loyal viewer base. Therefore, those who make reselling videos split the advertising dollars with fewer creators, making our CPM's higher. While there are hundreds of thousands of makeup tutorial videos, there may be less than 100 videos about how to list items for sale on Poshmark.

I have been fortunate that my CPM's have been on the higher side throughout my YouTube career. The average CPM is only $4 per 1,000 views, but it varies between every channel and can change daily. My CPM's are always changing, going up and down depending on the money advertisers are investing in YouTube ads.

Once your YouTube videos are monetized to earn AdSense revenue, you can track your CPM in your account's YouTube Studio area. Simply click on the **Analytics** tab on the left side of the page to see your AdSense totals (you can customize the date range), and then click on **Revenue** to see your CPM.

However, while your CPM number is important, your RPM, which stands for Revenue Per Mile, is the amount of money you are actually earning. This metric represents how much money YouTube is actually paying you per 1,000 video views via Ads, Channel Memberships, YouTube Premium revenue, Super Chats, and Super Stickers (will discuss each of these further along in this chapter).

CPM is the cost per 1000 ad impressions BEFORE YouTube takes their cut. RPM is your total revenue per 1000 views AFTER YouTube takes their cut. While your CPM is an advertiser-focused metric that only includes income from the ads on your videos on videos that are monetized, RPM is a creator-focused metric that provides for total revenue reported from all available sources. It also includes the total number of views from your videos. Your RPM number will always be lower than your CPM number as it is calculated after YouTube's revenue share and because it includes all views, even those on videos that, for whatever reason, were not monetized.

Confused? Don't worry, most people are! To be honest, I myself rarely dig too deeply into these numbers. I focus on tracking my revenue share in the **YouTube Studio section** of my YouTube account (simply click on your profile picture in the top right-hand side of your YouTube account and select "YouTube Studio" from the menu to find yours). By clicking on the **Analytics** icon on the left-hand side of the page, you will be able to bring up your **Channel Analytics**. From here, you can see your current revenue as well as several other statistics. You can also choose the date range, including:

- Last seven days
- Last 28 days
- Last 90 days
- Last 365 days
- Lifetime
- Current year
- Previous year
- Each of the past three months
- Custom

I personally narrow my display screen to the current month to see how my revenue is currently tracking. Selecting any of the time options will narrow down your statistics on an overview page where you can see your **Views, Watch time (hours), New subscribers,** and **Estimated revenue**. I like to narrow down my numbers by clicking on the Revenue tab to see my RPM and CPM. YouTube will also show you whether your numbers are up or down from the previous time-frame via red arrows.

Further down the page under **Revenue** are even more helpful insights and statistics, including your estimated revenue for each of the past six months along with your top-performing videos via revenue for the current month. You can also access your **Reach statistics** such as impressions, impressions click-through rate, views, and unique views. Under **Engagement**, you will find your watch time in hours and your average view duration. And finally, under **Audience**, you can see your unique viewers, average views per viewer, and the number of new subscribers.

All of these numbers, percentages, and statistics can be overwhelming. But the good thing is that you do not have to pay attention to them unless you enjoy digging through data. As I said, I only focus on my current running revenue balance and my CPM and RPM. And in truth, it is only my RPM revenue that is of any importance as that is how much money I will be paid.

Oh, and when do you get paid? **Once you have earned at least $100 via Google AdSense, Google will initiate a payment to you the following month.** So, you will get paid your January AdSense revenue in February, typically during the third week of the month.

AFFILIATE LINKS: While AdSense is the primary way most people earn money on YouTube, there is another way to bring in cash from your videos; and that is through affiliate links. When you sign up to be an affiliate with a company, you can access affiliate links that will pay you a commission whenever someone buys an item through your personal link.

Amazon offers the most popular referral program, called **Amazon Associates,** which many YouTubers use, as well as bloggers and social media influencers. I have been an Amazon Associate even before I started my YouTube channel. By signing up as an Amazon Associate, you can create referral links to any of the products on Amazon's website. Then if you use or mention a product in your video and provide a link to it in your YouTube video description box, you will earn a commission if anyone goes through your link to purchase that product.

Note that the person who clicks on your link does not have to purchase the exact product you link to; you will earn a commission on ANY items they buy once they are on Amazon's site if they got there using your referral link. With Amazon being the largest e-commerce site globally, it makes sense that most YouTube creators are also Amazon Associates, as it is an easy way to earn additional money. Go to any large YouTube channel. You will likely find several Amazon Associate links in the description boxes below their videos, most often for the equipment they are using to film their videos. Those $1000 DSRL cameras can earn you a hefty Amazon Associate commission if you link yours under your videos!

In addition to the Amazon Associate program, there are all kinds of companies that offer affiliate opportunities. In addition to Amazon, you can sign up to be an affiliate with:

- Adobe
- Airbnb
- Audible
- Brand Cycle
- Ebay Partner Network
- Honey
- LinkShare
- Movavi
- Shopify
- MySavings
- Sellfy
- ShareASale
- ShopHer Media
- ShopStyle
- Skillshare
- Skimlinks
- Tripadvisor
- Twitch

Another popular affiliate program is **Rakuten** (formerly "Ebates"). Rakuten is a shopping portal site that pays users a percentage back on their purchases. Shoppers simply create a free Rakuten account and then search the site for the retailer they want to shop from. They then click through to the store's website via Rakuten's link. Rakuten automatically tracks their spending, giving them a percentage back of their total purchase amount (anywhere from 1% up to 20%, depending on the site). Every three months, Rakuten automatically mails users out rebate checks. There are no points to track or special codes to enter; the entire process is automated on Rakuten's end.

While I utilize Rakuten for my own shopping rebates, I also use their affiliate program to make money. When you sign up for a Rakuten account, you are also given your own affiliate link to share on social media, including on YouTube. When someone signs up for Rakuten using your affiliate link and makes a purchase, you then earn $25. Any affiliate income you make is added to your own rebate total, and a check is then mailed out to you every three months. It is a safe, easy, and effective program to increase your overall YouTube earnings. And it is why you will see Rakuten affiliate links in many YouTube description boxes.

REFERRAL LINKS: While affiliate programs pay you in cash, referral programs reward you in products or in credits towards paying for your purchases. As an example, I belong to several monthly subscription box services, which I review on my YouTube vlog channel. If the company has a referral link, I will provide the link in the video's description box. Then if someone signs up for the subscription using my link, I earn rewards. Sometimes it is points toward free products; other times, it is free boxes.

Since affiliate programs pay in cash, I generally prefer them over referral links. However, some companies offer both; and it is then up to me to decide which reward is better. In some cases, I use the affiliate link to earn cash; but I use the referral link to earn free products in others. For instance, I have a subscription to Grove Collaborative, which is a membership-based website that sells eco-friendly household products. They have both an affiliate program and a referral program. I choose to use my referral link to use the credits towards buying my own cleaning supplies. To me, the credits are more useful than the affiliate money I could earn, even though the affiliate percentage is higher than the referral credit.

These days, nearly every brand and service seem to offer some type of referral program, including the major airlines and hotels, clothing and beauty companies, subscription boxes, and membership services. I belong to numerous referral programs, including FabFitFun, Cause Box, and Thrive Marketplace, just to name a few. Whenever you show an item of yours in a video, say a piece of clothing or a kitchen accessory, visit the brand's website to see if they offer an affiliate or referral program so that when you link the product in your video, you'll have the potential to earn either cash or credit!

SPONSORSHIPS: In addition to earning money through AdSense, Amazon Associates, Rakuten, affiliate links, and referral links, you can also bring in cash through sponsorships. A sponsorship is when a company pays you to film a video. If a company has a product to promote, they will send you the item and pay you to film a video about it. If it is a service, the company will pay you to talk about their company.

A major cosmetic brand recently sponsored me. They sent me a box of their makeup to review, and I filmed a video of me testing it out. On top of giving me free products, they also paid me a sponsorship fee. Note that you need to disclose sponsored videos, both verbally within the video and in the video's description box.

The more subscribers a channel has, the more lucrative sponsorships can be. Many large YouTube channels make more money from sponsorships than they do from AdSense. It takes a while to build up a large enough audience to start attracting sponsors; I began receiving sponsorship offers when my channel hit 5,000 subscribers (although I started getting offers of free products when my second channel barely had 1,000 subscribers). But it depends on what kind of content you are producing and how many actual views your videos typically get. Most brands will judge your channel based on the average number of views your videos receive, not necessarily by your subscriber numbers.

While most sponsorships come from companies contacting creators directly, you can also sign up with sponsorship companies to connect you with potential sponsors. These companies include, but are not limited to:

- AspireIQ
- Channel Pages
- Famebit
- Grapevine
- Izea
- Reelio
- Social BlueBook
- TapInfluence

A critical part of sponsorships is settling on the amount of money you expect to be paid. If you are just starting out, you cannot expect a company to pay you thousands of dollars to sponsor a video. In fact, in the early days of your YouTube career, you may only be able to film videos in exchange for free products.

However, as your channel grows, you can start to expect payment for your services. Most brands will try to pay you as little as possible, if anything at all; so, you must go into YouTube with the mindset that your time is valuable. If a company approaches you with a sponsorship offer, it is because they feel you are a good fit for their brand. Therefore, they should already expect that they will need to pay you to film a sponsored video for them.

While sponsors look at your total subscriber count, they also look at how many views your videos average. How much you will be comfortable charging is a question only you can answer, although a good formula to start with is $0.05 to $0.15 per view or $50 to $150 per 1,000 views. Some brands will ask you for your rate, while others will propose a fixed price. In the end, only you can decide the rate you will charge.

You must have policies in place before accepting a sponsorship deal. You want to agree on:

1. When will the video go live?
2. How long will the video need to be in terms of length?
3. Does the brand need to approve the video before it launches?
4. When and how will you receive your payment?
5. Will the company be providing you with a script?
6. Will the company be providing you with links to share with your viewers?
7. Will you be given free products to show in your video?
8. What else does the company expect from you? For example, will you be expected to share the video on social media?
9. Will the company be requiring that you use specific hashtags?
10. Will the company be providing you with disclosure text to place in the description box of the video?

Some companies will ask very little of you other than filming a video discussing their product or service, while others will expect you to sign a contract and complete numerous steps in order to get paid. I have had some brands just mail me a product to show in a video while others have demanded I sign a contract with very detailed instructions on how, what, where, and when to film. The more a company expects of you, the more you should expect from them in terms of compensation.

SELLING YOUR OWN PRODUCTS: From tee shirts and coffee mugs to courses and books, YouTube creators frequently sell their own merchandise, also called "merch." My YouTube channel drives traffic to my books (in addition to this book, I have written several books about selling on Ebay) and to my Ebay store, and I also have print-on-demand items that I sell, both on Amazon and TeePublic. I provide links to all my products in the description boxes below every video I post in hopes that some of my viewers will purchase my products. I do not think I would be as successful as I have been with my books if it was not for YouTube.

Creating your own merchandise is easy on sites like TeePublic and TeeSpring. I create my designs using Canva software. I have a TeePublic store that is linked under my YouTube videos, and I sell items ranging from tee-shirts to coffee mugs there every week. I also have merchandise that I have created in TeeSpring that appears below my videos. If you have a nickname or tag-line, considering slapping it on a tee-shirt and offering it up for sale to your YouTube viewers to help grow your brand and bring in extra money.

CHANNEL MEMBERSHIPS: Channel memberships are a relatively new feature for YouTube creators. Memberships allow viewers to join your channel through monthly payments, enabling them to receive perks such as special emojis, badges, stickers, and more.

Note that there is a minimum eligibility requirement that creators must meet before being able even to apply to offer Channel Memberships. As of this writing, requirements include:

- Your channel must have more than 30,000 subscribers (gaming channels only need more than 1,000 subscribers)
- Your channel must be enrolled in the YouTube Partner Program
- You must be over 18 years of age
- You must be located in one of the eligible countries Argentina, Australia, Austria, Bahrain, Belarus, Belgium, Bolivia, Bosnia and Herzegovina, Brazil, Bulgaria, Canada, Chile, Colombia, Costa Rica, Croatia, Cyprus, Czech Republic, Denmark, Dominican Republic, Ecuador, El Salvador, Estonia, Finland, France, Germany, Greece, Guatemala, Honduras, Hong Kong, Hungary, Iceland, India, Indonesia, Ireland, Israel, Italy, Japan,

Kuwait, Latvia, Lebanon, Liechtenstein, Lithuania, Luxembourg, Macedonia, Malaysia, Malta, Mexico, Netherlands, New Zealand, Nicaragua, Norway, Oman, Panama, Paraguay, Peru, Philippines, Poland, Portugal, Qatar, Romania, Russia, Saudi Arabia, Senegal, Serbia, Singapore, Slovakia, Slovenia, South Africa, South Korea, Spain, Sweden, Switzerland, Taiwan, Thailand, Turkey, Uganda, United Arab Emirates, United Kingdom, United States, Uruguay, Vietnam)

- Your channel is not set as made for children
- Your channel does not have a significant number of in-eligible videos (such as set as being made for kids or with music claims)

If you are eligible and choose to offer Channel Memberships to your viewers, you can select from several "perks" to features, including:

- Badges
- Emojis
- Private videos
- Live chats
- Downloads of content
- In-per meetings
- Contests
- Sweepstakes

Some creators also offer physical items that they mail out to their channel members, such as stickers, cards, shirts, and more. You can offer memberships priced as low as $0.99 per month all the way up to $99.99 a month. Creators receive 70% of membership revenue after applicable taxes, and fees are taken out.

YOUTUBE PREMIUM: YouTube Premium is a subscription service that costs $11.99 per month and allows viewers to:

- Watch videos ad-free
- Download videos to watch offline

- Play videos in the background while using other apps
- Access the YouTube Music App
- Listen to music ad-free
- Download music to listen to offline
- Play music in the background while using other apps
- Ad-free YouTube Kids videos as well as the ability to play offline
- Google Play Music for most countries

Creators do not have to subscribe to YouTube Premium for their videos to be included in the subscription. And while ads will not be appearing on your videos if someone with a You-Tube Premium account is viewing them, you will still receive a cut of the membership fees that are being paid to YouTube by subscribed viewers.

SUPER CHATS & SUPER STICKERS: Super Chats and Super Stickers allow viewers to connect with creators during live chats. Viewers can purchase Super Chats to send creators money; their comment then appears highlighted in the chat. Viewers can also purchase Super Stickers, which are a digital or animated image that pops up in the live chat feed. Channels with many subscribers can often earn quite a bit of money from viewers sending them these chats and stickers during live stream videos. For those with huge channels, a Super Chat is often the only way for a viewer to be noticed by a creator during a live stream as the creator will hear a notification sound when they receive a donation as well as the comment or sticker being highlighted in the chat stream.

PATREON: Patron is a membership service that some YouTube creators utilize to earn additional income. Some channels use Patreon essentially like a tip jar, while others have multiple membership levels, each with varying degrees of perks such as exclusive videos and merchandise.

TIP JAR: Just as some creators use Patreon as a virtual tip jar, you can also collect tips on your blog, website, or YouTube channel via several ways, including by providing your audience with your PayPal, Stripe, or Venmo email. A simple message such as "If you would like to support my channel with a virtual "tip," you can send it to:_____" with the email address associated with your account.

FUN FACTS

Current Top YouTube Earners:

1. Ryan's World (toy reviews) - $26 million
2. Dude Perfect (tricks and stunts) - $20 million
3. Like Nastya (toy reviews) - $18 million
4. Jeffree Star (beauty) - $17 million
5. DanTDM (gaming) - $16.5 million
6. PewDiePie (gaming) - $15.5 million
7. VanossGaming (gaming) - $15.5 million
8. Logan Paul (pranks) - $14.5 million
9. Markiplier (gaming) - $13 million
10. Jake Paul (pranks) - $11.5 million

CHAPTER FIVE:

MARKETING

If you really want to establish a presence on YouTube and earn money from your videos, you will have to do everything you can to promote your channel and build your brand. YouTube is a social media platform, and you want to use all the other social media sites available to you to draw traffic to your videos. More traffic equals more views, which in turn equals more AdSense revenue, and that can also lead to sponsorship opportunities as your channel grows. Fortunately, the social media sites that will bring you the most traffic are all free and easy to use. And it is likely that you already have accounts on some or even all of them.

Setting up your various social networking sites is yet another reason why it is so essential that you choose the best YouTube channel name possible right out of the gate. You want to be known under the same name everywhere to establish your brand. I am "Ann Eckhart" on my blog and YouTube channel we well as on Facebook, Twitter, Instagram, and Pinterest. I use the same logo across all my sites, too, so that no matter what website someone is browsing, when they see "Ann Eckhart" and my logo, they know it is me. My second channel may be called "Ann Eckhart Vlogs," but I still promote it under my "Ann Eckhart" brand as it is just easier to have one social media account identity across each of the various sites.

While I do YouTube for fun, it is also a business for me. Everything I create in regards to my channel is done to promote it as a brand. My videos drive traffic to my blog, and my blog drives traffic to my videos, and both the blog and videos drive traffic to my books. My blog and my videos both earn me AdSense money; so, having them essentially working together increases my ad revenue. My social networking accounts draw traffic to my blog and YouTube, resulting in more AdSense dollars. And all of my sites work to help me sell books, bring in sponsorships, and earn affiliate income and referral credits.

BLOG/WEBSITE: Most successful YouTube creators have coordinating blogs or websites, some even starting those sites before creating YouTube channels. What is great about a blog or a website is they are additional ways to earn AdSense dollars. When you have both a blog and a monetized YouTube channel, you have two AdSense income sources. Plus, you can place other ads on your site, some through affiliate and referral programs and others directly from selling advertising to companies.

Before I started my current blog (originally called *SeeAnnSave* but now at *Ann Eckhart.com*), I had dabbled in blogging a few different times on Blogger, which is Google's blog platform. I originally had a blog dedicated solely to my Ebay business. However, when I started *AnnEckhart.com*, I closed the former blog and moved all content to my new website.

The difference between that old Ebay blog and my current *AnnEckhart.com* blog is that my Ebay blog was just a blog, whereas my AnnEckhart.com blog is technically a website that hosts my blog. So now, I have a blog ON a website.

Confused? Do not worry; I was, and still am sometimes, when trying to explain the difference! Even today, I struggle with whether to call *AnnEckhart.com* a blog or a website. In the beginning, I called it a website, but these days I call it a blog, even though it is technically a website, mainly because the term "blog" is more prevalent in the social media world. Oy!

To put it simply, a blog that is on a free platform such as Blogger or WordPress is just a blog. However, a website is an actual site that you own that utilizes blogging software. *AnnEckhart.com* is my website, and on my website, I use WordPress blogging software.

When you have a blog on a free site, it is not yours but instead belongs to the company behind the site you are using, which means that it could be shut down at any time, resulting in you losing all your content. And while Blogger and WordPress have been around for years and show no signs of going anywhere, the risk is still there that you could eventually lose all your content.

I have my blog set up through Bluehost (bluehost.com), and I use WordPress software. This is a different set up than just starting a free blog on a site such as Blogger or WordPress. Since I am using a hosting company, I actually OWN my website. I pay Bluehost for all their hosting services and features, one of which is the WordPress blogging software. I decided to go the route of paying for my site so that it could not be taken down. If Blogger or WordPress were to suddenly shut down (not likely to happen, of course, but you never know), I would still have my website as I own it through a hosting company.

Having an actual website that incorporates a blogging platform also allows me many more options for customization. I could do a lot more with my Bluehost site than I could if I were going directly through WordPress, for example. Bluehost offers numerous free plug-ins for my site, including those for placing AdSense ads. I simply installed one of the free AdSense plug-ins, clicked where I wanted ads to show, and the ads were automatically placed. I now earn AdSense money from those ads. And I can change the ad placements and sizes at any time.

I look at my website as my "homepage" for everything I do. I can share my videos there as well as my books. I can post updates, which automatically go out to anyone who subscribes to receive them. I have my affiliate and referral links organized along with links to all of my social media pages. I even have an entire section devoted to my recipes, which are very popular with my followers. When I speak with someone who asks about my YouTube channel or books, it is much easier for me to direct them the *AnnEckhart.com* than it is trying to explain how they can find my YouTube channel or my books on Amazon. *AnnEckhart.com* is the leading portal for my "brand."

While having a coordinating blog or website can be helpful, note that it is not this book a requirement. Many successful YouTube creators do not have any sort of website. While they may utilize some additional social media sites to promote themselves, many focus solely on their channel. In fact, there are quite a number of successful YouTube creators who ONLY utilize YouTube. And when you are just starting out, that certainly makes the most sense. Start with YouTube and the other social media sites before deciding when or even if you need a dedicated blog or website.

When I had my Ebay blog on Blogger, I did not put anything significant on it; I just posted about new listings in my store and had the links to my social networking sites. I rarely even promoted the blog; I just maintained it so that if anyone happened to stumble across it, they would hopefully click through to my Ebay store.

However, my *AnnEckhart.com* blog is a business for me as I earn income through affiliate advertising and referral links, not to mention that it drives traffic to my YouTube channel and to my books. If my current site was on a free blogging platform, all of my information could be lost in a moment's notice. However, as long as I keep paying my website maintenance fees, my content is safe and belongs to me.

I personally would not even bother creating a blog on a free platform as you do not want to spend time driving traffic to a site that you might eventually want to change. If you are absolutely sure that you want to start your own site, I would go straight to a paid version so that you own it right out of the gate. A website is something that can wait until you are further along in your YouTube career.

If you decide to go with a paid website, do your research as there are many companies out there to choose from. I went with a large company (bluehost.com) because I wanted my blog to be the centerpiece of my brand and because I wanted to utilize several forms of affiliate advertising on it. However, there are a lot of low-cost website options out there. For instance, you can not only register for website URL's on GoDaddy (godaddy.com), but they also offer website hosting along with easy-to-create websites and blogs.

So, which should you choose? A free blog or a website? Or no site at all? That is a decision only you can make. Having a blog or website for your YouTube channel is NOT a requirement. In fact, it may be more work than is worth it for you. And as I talk about in the next section, you may find that a Facebook page can just as easily act as your "website."

However, if you do decide to set up a blog or website, it does not have to be complicated. Think of it as the "home" page for your brand to provide the links to your videos and all your social networking sites.

One significant benefit of having a blog is that you can run giveaways there. YouTube no longer allows you to host giveaways on your channel or videos. You are not allowed to tie in giveaway requirements to your videos, meaning you cannot instruct people to enter a giveaway by subscribing to your channel, giving a video a "thumbs up," or leaving a comment. You can announce giveaways in your videos, but you must direct people somewhere else to enter.

Hence, a website comes in handy for hosting giveaways as people can enter directly on your site. When I do a giveaway, I first write up a post detailing the prize and entrance requirements, and people enter by leaving comments on the post. I then randomly draw the winner or winners from the entries. Or I sometimes use a site such as Random.org to insert code that allows people to enter the giveaway quickly and makes it easy for me to draw the winner. Because people must submit their email addresses to enter the giveaways, I just email the winner to obtain their mailing address to send them their prize.

It is important to note that Facebook has the same policy as YouTube regarding giveaways in that you cannot run them on their site. If you plan to do giveaways, you will need to have a site other than YouTube or Facebook to host them. You can, however, run the giveaways on Twitter or Instagram.

Note that in addition to posting updates on your blog, you will also need to maintain it. If you allow visitors to leave comments on your posts, you will want to make sure to respond to them. You also want to maintain all links to ensure they are active and up-to-date so that people do not click through and get an error.

You will also want to secure a URL or several URLs for your website. I use GoDaddy.com to purchase my URL's; I own not only *AnnEckhart.com* but also several iterations of my name as well as my Ebay store and other businesses I own. It is an added expense to purchase URL addresses, but if you are serious about building a brand, it is an investment you will want to make.

FACEBOOK: If you want to "brand" yourself and your YouTube channel, you will want to set up a Facebook page. Facebook offers more ways to connect with your audience than Twitter, Pinterest, and Instagram combined. And if you do not want the hassle of maintaining a blog, a Facebook page can efficiently act as your dedicated "website."

YouTube makes it easy to share your videos to Facebook as there is a Facebook "share" button located under all videos. Simply click on the Facebook icon, link your YouTube and Facebook accounts together, and you can then share your YouTube videos on your personal and/or business page.

Note that while you may have a personal Facebook account, you will want to set up a Facebook PAGE for your YouTube channel. A Facebook business page is different from a personal Facebook page, although you first need to have a personal Facebook account and page to set up a business page.

A business page is one people "like," while a personal page is one where people "friend" you. A personal Facebook page has a limit on the number of "friends" you can have, but you can have limitless "likes" on your business page. Having a business page also allows you to separate your personal and public life. My personal Facebook page is private and is only for my personal friends and family to see. However, my Ann Eckhart Facebook page is public; anyone can view it and "like" it in order to be notified when I post there. Since my public page is a business page, it also allows me to accept sponsorships from companies that pay me to post about their products.

As your YouTube channel grows, you will likely find that viewers want to "friend" you on your personal Facebook page. Even if you are not promoting your personal page, it will still be easy for most people to find. Unless it is a subscriber you have gotten to know very well, I strongly encourage you NOT to add subscribers as friends on Facebook. You want to maintain privacy with a division between your personal and public/business life. While many of my friends and family do "like" my Facebook business page, not all do. Keeping my personal page private protects me and my friends and family from having their information exposed to my business page's followers.

I use my Facebook business page to promote my YouTube videos and books, and I save my personal information for my personal Facebook account. While it is hard to turn down friend requests from well-meaning people, I only accept Facebook "friend" requests from my actual friends and family for safety and security reasons. YouTube subscribers and readers of my books need to "like" my Facebook business page to connect with me.

I have set up my personal Facebook page with the tightest security settings to protect myself. I have turned off the private messaging settings on my business page so that people cannot send me messages. When I allowed people to message me, I found myself inundated with long notes from people wanting advice on Ebay, help with publishing, or just someone to chat with. While most of these messages were harmless, it took a lot of my time and energy to deal with all the questions.

Again, just as it is hard to deny friend requests, it can be hard to ignore messages from well-meaning followers. However, I always remind myself that I am not just running my YouTube channel for fun but also for profit. I am growing my brand for the long term, and I need to treat it as a business. I also need to protect myself and my family by guarding my personal information as much as possible.

A Facebook page needs "likes" to grow. While it can take a while to build up the number of "likes" on a business page, I still believe it is essential to set one up separate from your personal account. I have seen many people start out using their personal Facebook account for their online content, only to reach the maximum number of "friends" allowed eventually. They then had to scramble to create a business page and encourage everyone to "like" it. Facebook users are more accustomed to "friending" people than "liking" pages, so it does take longer to build a business page than a friend list.

To set up a Facebook business page, simply visit **facebook.com/about/pages.** You will need to log into your personal Facebook account first, and then the system will walk you through the steps necessary to create your business page. Creating a Facebook business page is free and easy to do, and I consider it an essential step in establishing your brand and building your YouTube channel.

The first decision you will need to make is to **name your business Facebook page**. My Facebook business page is *Ann Eckhart,* the same name as my blog and YouTube channel, not to mention my author name and the name I use on my other social media accounts. You will want your page name to match your YouTube channel name, too.

As you go forward with creating more social media accounts, you will again want your name to be the same across all platforms. Remember, the goal is to BRAND yourself so that people will recognize you on all forms of social media. Therefore, now is the time to make sure you are happy with your channel name.

There are all kinds of things you can personalize on your Facebook page. You want to add a profile picture and a banner. I have a headshot as my profile picture, and I make my own customized banners for social media on apps like Canva and WordSwag. Whatever photos or graphics you choose, remember that this is your BUSINESS page, so keep it professional. You do not want to post potentially controversial photographs of yourself; look at other YouTube creators' Facebook pages to get an idea of the kinds of photos and graphics that are acceptable to share.

You will also want to fill out the extensive **About** section of your page to provide people with information about your YouTube channel. However, since this is your BUSINESS page and separate from your personal page, you will want to be careful with how much information you share. While you may have your cell phone number available on your personal page to keep in touch with family and friends, unless you have a brick-and-mortar location that you want people to call, you will want to leave that section blank on your business page.

You will first need to choose the **Category** for your page; as a YouTube creator, there are several categories you can choose from, such as "Public Figure," "Entertainer," or "Personal Blog or Website." I prefer the latter; please do not dub yourself as a public figure or celebrity until you have reached at least a million subscribers. Touting yourself as something other than you are will turn off potential followers. You will need to select a sub-category, too. And do not worry about being locked into your selections; you can easily change them at any time. In fact, Facebook regularly updates the options, so it is always good to check them a couple of times a year to see if better selections have been added.

In addition to your **Name** (the name of your page, i.e., your YouTube channel name), you can edit your Facebook URL so that it ends in that name. This provides you with a clickable URL link that you will want to provide on both your YouTube channel "About" section as well as in the description box under all of your videos.

Once you have created your Facebook business page, you will be able to fill in the **About** section. Here you can enter in your **Location**, although I keep this field blank to protect my privacy. Next up are **two description fields,** one short and one long. I have one simple sentence in the first field (Ann Eckhart is an author, YouTube content creator, and Ebay seller based in Iowa.). I provide a bit more information in the second field (*Welcome to the official Facebook page of Ann Eckhart (formerly SeeAnnSave)! I am an author, vlogger, influencer, and Ebayer. I am also a pug dog mom, caregiver, and Walt Disney World fanatic!*). Again, you can edit these fields at any time, so don't worry about being locked into what you first type in.

Next, you will see **your pages' statistics**, including how many people "like" your page and how many people "follow" the page. Underneath these numbers will be a **field to enter one website URL.** If you are creating your Facebook page specifically to promote your YouTube channel, you will want to put your channel URL into this field. I have my Amazon Author Page linked here, but regardless, you will be able to further link your other sites down on the page.

In the next section, you can enter a **phone number**; however, you should leave this field blank unless you want strangers to call you. There are also fields for you to post your **email address** (I have a business email that I share across all of my accounts; I just use the one that I set up in Google when I started my YouTube channel), **additional categories** (these are Facebook's versions of "tags"; I choose "writer," "author," and "video creator"); and finally, there is space to post **all of your other links** (I have links to my blog, Instagram, Twitter, and both of my YouTube channels here).

You will also want to take some time to customize your page's **Settings**, the link for which can be found on the left side of your page. There are lots of options available for you to edit here; I am going to share with you what mine are and why I choose them

- **Page Visibility:** Page published (obviously as my page is public on Facebook!)
- **Visitor Posts:** Disable posts by other people on the page (I choose this setting to prevent anyone from sharing their posts on my page; this is mainly done to control spam and trolls.)
- **Post and Story Sharing:** Allow Sharing To Stores (This allows my followers to share my posts with their Facebook friends, which can help me gain more followers and/or clicks through to my Amazon Author Page and YouTube channels.)
- **Audience Optimization for Posts** (I personally left

this blank)

- **Messages:** I do not allow people to contact my Page privately by showing them the Messaging buttons. This is a personal decision; if you feel comfortable having your followers message you through Facebook, then you can select this option.
- **Tagging Ability:** I do not allow others to tag photos and videos published by my page to maintain control over my content.
- **Others Tagging This Page:** I do not allow these options for the same reason of maintaining control over my content.
- **Country Restriction:** I have none
- **Age Restrictions:** I choose Public, but there are also options for ages 17 and up, 18 and up, 19 and up, 21 and up, and Alcohol-Related.
- **Page Moderation:** I left this field blank, but you can block posts or comments that contain specific words.
- **Profanity Filter:** I have this turned Off, but you can also select from Medium or Strong.

- **Similar Page Suggestions:** I selected for my page to be include when recommending similar Facebook Pages that people might like on a Page timeline.
- **Page Updates:** I selected to publish posts when info is uploaded on my page automatically.
- **Post in Multiple Languages:** I have this turned off as I only know English!
- **Translate Automatically:** However, I have selected for Facebook to show people who understand other languages' automatic translations of my posts when available.
- **Comment Ranking:** I choose for Facebook to show me the most relevant comments by default.
- **Content Distribution:** I have not chosen to prohibit

downloading to Facebook.

Finally, there are options to **Download Page** and **Merge Page**, providing you with links to complete those tasks if you so desire (I have never used these). And the last option is to **Remove Page**, which will delete your page so that nobody will see it or find it. If you ever select to delete your page, you will have 14 days to restore it if you change your mind.

Once you have your Facebook business page set up, it is time to start building your audience by getting people to "Like" your page. You will be able to invite friends and family on your personal page to "Like" your new business page. And of course, you can promote your Facebook page on your YouTube channel by adding your page URL to the "About" section on YouTube as well as providing the link under all of your videos.

Once you have a Facebook page and other social media accounts, you will want to make sure to provide links to all your pages in the information section of your YouTube channel home page and under each video. Note that you need to enter the full URL address of your sites, including the "http://" as only the http links will be active, allowing viewers to click through to the sites directly. I have my full description bar write up and links in a Word document that I simply copy and paste into the description box of every video I upload. I will discuss this further in *Chapter Seven: A Day in the Life.*

As I mentioned earlier, I use my blog and all my social networking accounts together. When I upload a new YouTube video, I post the link to Facebook. Unfortunately, Facebook has made it increasingly difficult for people to see posts, hiding posts from business pages as they want those of us with pages to pay for the posts to be seen.

You have likely noticed the **Boost** buttons under posts that encourage you to pay for your updates to be directly shown to your followers. And while it can be tempting to spend $5 or more to ensure your posts are seen, resist the urge to boost everything you put on Facebook as the results are not worth the cost. Instead, perhaps spend $5 every other week or so to promote one post to see if it affects your page "likes" and/or on your YouTube subscriber growth.

Because Facebook is selective about what posts they will show your followers, it is essential to do more than just post links to your Facebook page to engage your audience. Facebook prefers original posts and photos over links that you simply copy and paste to your page. I try to post a regular status update at least once a day, which is more likely to be shown to my followers than a post with a link that I share directly from my blog. I also occasionally share photos on my Facebook page; like status updates, pictures tend to show up to more people than just links to my blog. Since my Facebook and Instagram accounts are linked, it is easy to share whatever I post to Instagram to Facebook. That way, I can knock out two social media posts with just one step.

Another way to engage your Facebook page users is to post "teasers" for upcoming videos. Post a photo of yourself as you are prepping to film, or a picture of something you are getting ready to share, with the message that a new video will be coming the next day. This will get people excited about your latest video to be released.

You want to encourage people to "like" and "comment" on your Facebook posts in the hopes their activity will show up on their friends' feeds, which will help more people come to your page. You have likely seen this happen on your Facebook feed, where it will show you that a friend liked a post or a page. The convenient "like" thumbs up icon will be there, making it easy for you, too, to "like" the page.

It is always my hope that when someone "likes" one of my posts that their friends will see it, check out my page, and then "like" it, too. As I mentioned earlier, Facebook shows status updates and photos more than links; so, I get more "likes" and comments on my status updates and pictures than I do when I simply share links to my blog posts or videos.

As I mentioned earlier, you may decide that a Facebook page can act like your blog or website rather than setting up a separate site. Many YouTube creators do not have a blog or website, preferably using Facebook as their homepage. So, unless you have the time to devote to maintaining a separate website, consider just using Facebook along with other social networking to promote your Ebay business. I recommend you do Facebook FIRST as you can always add a blog/website later.

TWITTER: If you do not already have a Twitter account, you can create one at **Twitter.com.** If you do have an account that you are active on, consider creating a new one just for your YouTube channel. As with Facebook, you want to keep your personal and business lives separate on Twitter. Make sure your Twitter handle is the same as your YouTube channel. Remember, part of branding is being known as ONE name across ALL social media platforms. You will need a different email address for each Twitter account you create; since you were given a Gmail address when you signed up for a Google account, you can use that one.

Like Facebook, Twitter provides a free and easy way to connect with viewers and drive traffic to your YouTube videos. YouTube makes sharing your videos to Twitter super easy as there is a Twitter share button under all videos. Simply click on the Twitter icon and link your YouTube account to your Twitter account to share the title of your video, as well as the direct link and the thumbnail of your video.

Twitter allows users to share posts of 140 characters or less. While your video's title and the link will automatically be put into the Twitter field, you can increase your exposure by adding hashtags. **Hashtags** are simply keywords that follow a pound (#) sign. For instance, when I film a video about selling on

Ebay, I will use hashtags such as:

- #ebay
- #ebayseller
- #reselling
- #makingmoneyonline
- etc.

I try to add as many hashtags as I have room for as savvy Twitter users search for tweets using hashtags, which increases the chance of you driving traffic to your videos.

I set aside some time every evening to connect with other Twitter users since I can do this on my iPhone while relaxing in front of the TV. I follow other bloggers and YouTube creators, retweet posts I like, reply to posts, and post a Tweet or two of my own. Twitter works best when you actively engage with other users, so it is crucial to spend some time each day networking on Twitter so that you can grow your followers.

Some Twitter users follow everyone who follows them, which can certainly be a way to build up your followers. You can also "network" with other folks on Twitter by replying to, retweeting, or favoring tweets. As I mentioned when setting up your Facebook page, you can add all your social media links, including your Twitter URL, in the "About" section of your Facebook business page; so hopefully, some of your Facebook fans will follow you to Twitter. To encourage this, about once a week, post your Twitter link directly to your Facebook page to make it easy for people to click through and "follow" you.

Add your Twitter URL to the list of other links you share on your YouTube channel, both in your channel information section as well as under each video. Remember to add the http:// to your link to make it active so that users can directly click through to your Twitter account.

The **Edit Profile** feature located on your Twitter homepage allows you to customize the look and information people will see when they click on your profile. Add a nice, clear photo of yourself (or your logo, if you have one); and add a header image. Write up a brief but fun description of yourself. Put the link to your YouTube channel in the website field so that people can click through to your videos. And finally, click on "theme colors" to customize your profile page even further.

Personalizing your Twitter profile and then engaging with other users every day will increase people finding your You-Tube videos and subscribing to your channel, therefore earning you more AdSense revenue!

PINTEREST: Pinterest is often overlooked when it comes to promoting YouTube videos, but, as with Facebook and Twitter, it is another free and easy way to drive traffic to your channel and increase your video views. And increased views mean more AdSense dollars!

If you don't already have a Pinterest account, you can create one at **pinterest.com**. If you are already an active Pinterest user, you can just do what I have done and add a "YouTube Videos" board to your account.

Pinterest allows you to create boards, where you pin content. You can "pin" content that others have posted, and you can also share your own "pins." Pinterest started as a way for people, mainly women, to "pin" craft ideas and recipes to virtual boards. However, Pinterest is quickly becoming a tool for busi-nesses to get the word out about their products and develop brand loyalty. And as you grow your YouTube brand, you will want to make Pinterest a part of your marketing strategy.

I have a board on Pinterest that I have titled *YouTube Videos*. As with Facebook and Twitter, YouTube provides a "share" icon for Pinterest underneath all videos. After I upload a video to YouTube, I simply click on the Pinterest icon and "pin" it to my *YouTube Videos* board. The video then appears on the feed of those who follow me on Pinterest. They can click through to my video directly from my pin. And if they "repin" the post, then their followers will also see it. I have noticed a dramatic increase in my blog and YouTube traffic since I started pinning my blog posts and videos to Pinterest.

Just as you should be doing with your Facebook and Twitter links, be sure to link your Pinterest page in your YouTube channel profile as well as in the description bar underneath all your videos. And put the link in the General Information section of your Facebook page. Be sure to periodically share your Pinterest link on both Facebook and Twitter to attract new followers.

You may be noticing by now that a big part of social networking is to have all your sites working together. Include all your social media links on your blog/website and Facebook. Post your Twitter and Pinterest links to Facebook; share your Facebook and Pinterest links on Twitter. The more you can get your YouTube channel link out there, the easier it will be for people to find your videos and for your channel to grow!

INSTAGRAM: Instagram offers another free, easy, and fun way to interact with your YouTube subscribers and gain more viewers. In fact, in just the past year or so, Instagram brings my YouTube channel more traffic than Facebook, Twitter, and Pinterest combined. Instagram allows you to share photos and "like" and comment on photos shared by others. While you cannot put a full-length YouTube video on Instagram, you can share content and put in links to your channel, both with your photos and in your profile.

To create an Instagram account at **Instagram.com.** Again, make sure your Instagram name is the same as your YouTube channel and other social media sites. If you already have a personal Instagram account, consider creating a second one specifically for your YouTube channel and brand.

The best use of Instagram that I have found is to connect with subscribers on a more personal level. While I mainly talk about

Ebay and making money online on my YouTube videos, I share personal photos of my dogs and family on Instagram. I also post pictures of fun activities such as eating dinner out (Instagram users love food photos!) or attending local events. And I also post funny memes and jokes, which are always a hit and increase engagement. Whatever the photo content, however, the main goal is to further connect with followers who are interested in the content I am providing, whether it is on my YouTube channel or in the books I write.

Just like on Twitter, **hashtags** are a big part of getting your content on Instagram found. I like to include three to five hashtags with every photo I share. If I share a picture of an estate sale haul of items I plan to sell on Ebay, I will use hashtags such as:

- #ebay
- #estatesale
- #reselling
- #ebayseller
- #reseller
- etc.

You can create a long list of hashtags in the "notes" app on your phone and simply copy and paste them onto all of your posts. The goal of these hashtags is that many people will search for them and find me. Even if they do not follow me on Instagram, they still check out my profile and click through to my Amazon Author Page or my YouTube channel.

Instagram allows you to include one website link in your profile, but you can install tools that will enable you to create a bio link that houses a menu of all your other links. **Linktr.ee** is the most popular of these apps, but others include:

- Campsite
- Link In Profile
- LitUrls
- Manylink

- Lnk
- Tap Bio
- Linkr.in
- Linkkle

I personally use the free version of Linktr.ee and find it suitable for my needs. With it, I can provide a menu of links to my You-Tube channels, blog, Twitter account, Facebook page, and Amazon Author Page. Suppose you are unsure about downloading one of these extensions, and your only goal is to drive traffic to your YouTube videos. In that case, it is perfectly acceptable to provide your channel's link in your Instagram profile only. You can always switch over to Linktr.ee or an alternative at a later date.

When promoting my YouTube channel via Instagram, I post a thumbnail from my most recent video and encourage followers to head over to my channel to watch it. Since the link to my YouTube channel is in my Linktree menu, which is linked in my bio, I usually write: *"New video now live on my YouTube channel; direct link in my profile @ann_eckhart."* The "@" link will take users to my profile page where the active link to my Linktree menu, and therefore my YouTube channel, will be. Then the user simply clicks on my YouTube channel URL, taking them straight to my videos.

Once you reach 10,000 Instagram followers, you can add "swipe up" links into your Instagram stories. After I share about a new video on my main Instagram feed, I also post about it in my Instagram stories with a direct link to the video so that people can "swipe up" to watch it. I usually add a fun GIF swipe up graphic along with a song from Instagram's music list. I have found that using the "swipe up" feature to take people directly to my YouTube videos is the most valuable part of reaching 10,000 Instagram followers.

As with Twitter and Pinterest, it is a good idea to actively network with others on Instagram by following them back, "liking" their pictures and leaving comments. I like to spend about 10 minutes a day scrolling through my Instagram feed to check out what others are posting and engage with my favorite posts.

Note, also, that Instagram is an app. While you can see your Instagram feed, edit your profile, and add followers on a computer, you can only add your own posts using the app on your smartphone or tablet. Unlike Facebook and Twitter, which both work about the same on a cell phone or desktop computer, Instagram works best on mobile devices.

NETWORK WITH FELLOW YOUTUBERS: There is a fine line between networking with other YouTube creators to grow your channel and outright using them to help you. One of the most painful things I see new YouTubers do is BEGGING people to subscribe to their channel. They stalk the successful YouTube channels and leave comments asking the viewers of someone else's channel to sub their channel, too. Or worse, they send out private messages to the subscribers of other channels asking them to subscribe.

If you are creating quality content, there is no reason to beg for subscribers. In fact, it is so tacky and frowned upon nowadays that you will likely turn off potential viewers. However, there are ways that you can network with other YouTube creators that are beneficial for both you and them.

First, you want to SUPPORT other channels. Subscribe to the channels you actually like, give their videos a thumbs up, leave nice comments, and share their videos via your social networks (I like to share my favorite videos to both Twitter and Pinterest using the "share" buttons located under each video). Showing your support to other channels not only helps your favorite YouTube creators, but it will likely get you noticed by their subscribers, drawing people to your channel. Again, do these things because you want to support channels that you enjoy; you should help other creators without expecting that they will return the favor, especially if the channels are much larger than yours.

Suppose you develop a friendly "relationship" with another YouTuber (they are replying to your comments or noticing your Tweets). In that case, it is okay to mention that you also make videos casually. It is best to let these relationships develop naturally; just like in real life, genuine internet friendships are based on both parties having an equal amount of respect and admiration for one another.

Suppose you find another YouTube creator with the same number of subscribers as you have and who is creating similar content. In that case, you may want to suggest doing a collaboration video with them. Many YouTubers do "collabs," where they partner with another channel to create videos with similar themes. Ideas include sending each other boxes of goodies to open on camera, answering "tag" questions, or participating in group challenges. If you live in the same area, have gotten to know another creator well, and feel safe meeting them in person, you can even film videos together, posting a video to your respective channels and then directing viewers to go to the other channel watch the other video. For instance, I have seen several resellers get together to shop at flea markets or antique malls. They each "vlog" their experiences and post to their channels, encouraging their viewers to check out the other respective vlogs.

Collaboration videos help you make friends in the YouTube community; everyone benefits by encouraging viewers to check out all the participating channels. People who do collab videos link each other's channels in their video's description boxes, and the videos are then shared via everyone's respective social media accounts.

Create great content, support the channels you enjoy watching, utilize your social media accounts, and let the viewers and subscribers build naturally! After all, you want people to WATCH your videos, not just hit subscribe because they have been paid or guilted into doing so.

FUN FACTS

Current Top 12 Most Popular Social Media Sites:

1. Facebook
2. YouTube
3. Whatsapp
4. Messenger
5. WeChat
6. Instagram
7. TikTok
8. Linkedin
9. Snapchat
10. Twitter
11. Reddit
12. Pinterest

CHAPTER SIX:

BEST PRACTICES

Film quality and marketing are not enough when it comes to gaining viewers and subscribers. Follow these best practices to ensure your YouTube career is a success!

PAYING FOR SUBSCRIBERS: One thing you absolutely do NOT want to do is pay for people to subscribe to your YouTube channel. There are online companies that, for a price, will get people (usually automated computer "robots" or "bots") to subscribe to your channel. However, VIEWS are what create AdSense revenue, not subscribers. People who have been paid to subscribe to a channel will not actually watch the videos. Plus, some sites track YouTube channel subscribers, views, and revenue, so it is obvious when someone has paid for subscribers as there will be a sudden massive spike in their numbers. It can actually hurt your channel if you have a large number of subscribers but a low number of video views in comparison

CHANNEL DESIGN: When you log into YouTube, you can select **Your Channel** (click on your profile picture in the top left-hand corner, and it is the first option in the drop-down menu) to edit the design of your channel's homepage via the **Customize Channel** icon. Once on the Channel customization page, there are three sections you can work on: Layout, Branding, and Basic

Info.

Under the **Layout** tab, you can add a **Channel trailer for people who haven' subscribed.** This acts as a commercial or preview for anyone who comes to your channel but is not yet subscribed. You can also upload a **Featured video for returning subscribers** to give a special welcome back for your loyal viewers.

Under the **Branding** tab, you can change your **Profile picture,** which is the photo that appears on not just your channel page but also next to all of your videos and next to any comments you post on your videos or anyone else's. A Banner image appears across the top of your channel. You need to provide an image that measures 2048x1152 pixels and 6MB or less. There are a lot of free apps that can create these specialty images; I personally use a YouTube thumbnail apps that offers multiple sizes for social media graphics.

Finally, you can add a **Video watermark** that will appear on your videos in the video player's right-hand corner. An image that measures 150x150 pixels is recommended. The image must be a PNG, GIF (no animations), BMP, or JPEG file that is 1MB or less. My watermark is my YouTube channel logo.

Under the **Basic info** tab is where you can add all of the links to your social media accounts, along with a blog/website if you have one. First, there is a field to write your Channel description. Mine currently reads: *Hi, and welcome to my channel! My name is Ann, and on March 30, 2020, this channel became the home of The Reselling Report, my daily podcast-style news show for people who sell on Ebay, Amazon, Etsy, and Poshmark. In addition to being a reseller, I am also a self-published author of several books, both under my name and stationery products under my Jean Lee Publishing name.*

I also provide my business email address, although I specify that it is for business inquiries only, such as sponsorship and brand deal proposals. I had to include that warning to stop people from sending me personal emails; I was getting so many messages a day that it took away from my ability to get any work done. It is one of those "tough love" moves that you will find yourself having to make as your YouTube channel grows.

In addition to my email, I also include my P.O. box address for both PR and viewer mail. Having a P.O. box is another decision you will want to make if you plan to build your YouTube channel as you do not want to give out your home address to your viewers.

In the middle of the page is the **Links** section. Here is where you can add all of your other links. I currently have the following URL's linked: my blog, my Amazon store (this is where I have my books as well as a list of reselling supplies and household favorites), Facebook page, Twitter account, Instagram page, Pinterest board, and second YouTube channel.

The last two sections of the page are **Links on banner**, where you can choose one of your links actually to appear on your channel's banner, and **Contact info**, where you can provide your email address.

DESCRIPTION BOX: When you upload a video to YouTube, you need to create a title and put some information into the description box that is below each video. I will share what is in my description box in the next chapter of this book, "A Day in the Life." Your description box should give your viewers directions for what you want them to do, and the first thing should be the most important as it the only one viewers will initially see unless they expand the view to reveal everything written in the box.

Some YouTubers ask views to give their videos a thumbs-up, leave a comment, and subscribe as the first things in their description boxes. Since I am trying to drive traffic to my books, I list my Amazon Author Page first. Under that, I have all the links to my social networking sites, a bit about me, and my disclaimer. If I end my video by directing people to my social networking sites, I tell them that all my links are listed in the description box below and that they just must click on the down arrow to bring everything into view.

I keep the verbiage in the description box of my videos in a Word document to simply copy/paste the information whenever I upload a new video. Because viewers only see the first three lines of the description bar unless they click to expand it, it is vital to put your most crucial directive there. Make sure any websites you link have the full URL addresses so that they will be "live," i.e., so viewers can click on them and be taken directly to your site.

ENCOURAGING LIKES, COMMENTS & SUBSCRIPTIONS: While it may seem logical that people who watch and enjoy your videos will give them a "thumbs up," leave comments, and subscribe to your channel, most viewers will not give you any sort of feedback whatsoever. As I mentioned earlier, many people will find your videos through internet searches or by YouTube recommending your videos to them while watching another creator's channel. Most viewers do not even have YouTube accounts, so, while they can watch videos via the app or on their computers, they cannot respond to your videos in any way.

For viewers who do have a YouTube account, however, you want to encourage interaction as much as possible. YouTube offers those with a YouTube account the ability to "like" (i.e., click on the little "thumbs up" icon) videos; "dislike" (i.e., click on the small "thumbs down" icon), leave a comment on videos; subscribe to channels; add videos to a "favorites" list; and share videos to their social media accounts. Encouraging people to do any of the above helps to promote your videos as the friends and followers of those viewers will see their activity and possibly decided to subscribe to your channel, too.

At the end of most of my videos, I will ask people to leave me any questions or comments they might have. I will also ask that if they liked the video to "give it a thumbs-up." Finally, I suggest that they subscribe for more videos if they haven't already done so. Some YouTube creators ask for likes and subscribers at the beginning of their videos, and some even mention it in the middle. What you do is up to you; you can always play around with this to see what feels the most natural.

MONITORING COMMENTS: Having viewers leave comments on your videos is something every YouTuber appreciates...unless those comments are mean. While most comments on my videos are positive, a "hater" comes along and says something rude or nasty every now and again. The more views a video gets, the more likely it is that someone will eventually leave a negative comment on it. The large YouTube channels whose videos get millions of views have to deal with an enormous amount of hate, or "trolls," some of it so bad that it has driven successful YouTubers off the site.

Some YouTuber creators do not monitor the comments left on their videos, believing that free speech protects those who leave comments and also feeling that any comment, good or bad, is engagement that ultimately benefits their growth. While I am all for free speech, I believe it comes with consequences. And the result for someone leaving a negative comment on one of my videos is that I remove the comment and ban the person from my channel so that they can't interact with me on YouTube in any way (either by giving a video a thumbs down, leaving me a comment, or sending me a message). My YouTube channel is my personal space. I would not allow someone to come into my home and treat me poorly, so I will not let them be mean to me through YouTube.

Even if you do not get rude comments, you will likely get the occasionally "thumbs down." I am currently averaging about five dislikes on all my videos; I honestly think they are from people who subscribe to my channel so that they hit that "thumbs down" icon on my videos when they go live! While it is never a good feeling to see a dislike, realize that almost every person who makes YouTube videos gets them, and the more views a video gets, the more dislikes it will have. This is just the nature of YouTube, so try to accept it and move on, focusing on the likes and positive comments you do receive.

As I said, however, most people who leave comments are kind and supportive. I try my best to reply to anyone who leaves a comment on any of my videos, although I usually only do this for the first day or two after the video goes live. Even if I cannot leave a written reply, I try to give nice comments a "thumbs up" and click on the little heart icon next to their comment to let them know that I saw it. While YouTube used to send a message to you every time a new comment was left on one of your videos, they no longer do this. You do get a notification of activity on your videos whenever you log in (there will be a little red box next to the bell icon at the top of the page with the number of activities – likes, comments, shares, subscriptions – that are new). Still, it's now a lot harder to find and reply to comments, especially on older videos.

What I like to do is go to my **YouTube Studio** (click on your profile picture in the top right-hand corner of the page; it is the third selection in the drop-down menu). This takes me to my **Channel dashboard**, and on the left-hand side of the page are several options I can choose from, including **Comments**. Once I click on the comment's icon (which is a speech bubble), I am brought to a dedicated page where comments are listed in chronological order, which allows me to see the most recent comments that have been left. It is easy for me to reply or like the comments, delete any that are inappropriate, and check on those marked **Held for review** or **Likely spam**.

Often people will continue to leave comments on videos months or even years after they were first put up, and responding to those can be nearly impossible unless you go to the dedicated Comments page so that you can see the most recent comments that have been left. Do the best you can to reply to comments, or at least to acknowledge that you are reading all comments in your videos.

You want to continually let your audience know that you appreciate all their "likes" and comments. However, the most successful YouTube channels do eventually have to stop reading and replying to comments as it is too time-consuming. At most, I may get 50 comments on a video, but it is usually much less, so it is still manageable for me. It is a great goal to have it eventually have so many viewers and comments that you cannot keep up replying to them!

PRIVACY: When the internet first became available, people could hide anonymously behind their computers, posting whatever they wanted under screen names without anyone knowing who or where they were. However, social media, and especially YouTube, has changed that. Even if you decide to make videos where you do not appear on the screen, you will still expose yourself to the world. Therefore, it is important to take the proper safety and security measures.

Keep the exact location of your home to yourself. I only ever say that I live in Iowa; I do not mention the precise city. I do not show the front of my house. I have a P.O. Box set up for mail so that I do not have to give out my home address. I do not announce if I am going on vacation, not only so that people do not know I am not home but also know where I will be. Now, I am a small-time YouTuber, and these measures may seem extreme. However, it is the level of privacy that I am most comfortable with. I would rather be safe than sorry. Once you have exposed the city you live in or shown the front of your house, that information is online forever. Be extra careful when you are filming and even talking so that you do not give away too much of your privacy.

SCHEDULE & CONSISTENCY: If you are on YouTube to make

money and build your brand, you will want to keep a consistent schedule of uploading videos. Some people upload on a specific day of the week while others aim for a set number of videos per week. I am currently posting one video per week on my *The Reselling Report* channel. My vlog channel schedule is more sporadic. I try to upload there once a week, usually on Sundays. But I have also tried a three-day-a-week schedule on that channel. *The Reselling Report* is my main focus right now; my vlog channel is something I only do for fun.

No matter what my posting plans are, though, I try to keep my viewers updated as to my schedule. The subscribers on my *The Reselling Report* channel expect videos to go up at 8:00 am Central time every Friday morning. So, if something unexpected happens, such as illness or losing power, I still try to put up a notice that a video will not be going up. I can do this by posting on the Community tab on my YouTube channel, which will show up in my subscriber's feed. And I can also post about the schedule change on Facebook, Twitter, and Instagram.

Nothing is worse than subscribing to a new YouTube channel that promises frequent videos, only never to see them again. If you are going to be successful on YouTube, you MUST commit to it. You cannot upload a few videos, abandon your channel, and then wonder why you do not have any subscribers and are not making any money. Find a filming schedule that works for you and stick to it! I recommend starting out with one or two videos a week and building on that schedule if you want to. The biggest mistakes I have seen new creators make are trying to start a daily vlogging channel to get burned out and abandon their YouTube career altogether. You can always build on your posting schedule, but it is tough to cut back on it as once viewers expect videos at specific days and times, they become agitated if you take content away.

YouTube analytics and viewers prefer videos that are around 15 minutes in length. Unless you are filming a vlog-style video or doing a live question and answer session or hangout, any-thing longer than 15 minutes is usually too long for most people. However, putting up videos that are too short may not satisfy viewers. And if viewers do not watch your video, you will not earn any AdSense revenue. I watch channels that put up 10-minute videos and others that produce videos over an hour. Again, sticking to your guns and creating the con-tent that pleases you is the most important thing, regardless of video length. Just remember that videos need to be at least 10 minutes long to insert the Mid-Roll Ad Breaks we discussed earl-ier in this book. To maximize your AdSense income, you will want to aim for videos that are at least 10 minutes in length.

However, more important than the length of videos is the QUALITY of them. You do not need expensive camera equip-ment or editing software to produce quality YouTube videos (I film and upload videos on an iPhone). Still, you do want your videos to be clear, steady, and well lit. Speak up so viewers can hear you. Back sure you have a nice backdrop if you are filming a sit-down video. Do you best to provide your viewers with the kind of quality video you enjoy watching.

Before you upload your video and make it live, watch it back first to ensure it looks and sounds nice. I would rather reshoot a video or skip it altogether than upload one that is of poor quality. When I upload my videos, I have them set to "Private" so that I can review them on YouTube before I make them pub-lic. And as my filming has gotten better over the years, I have deleted old videos that were not up to my standards and reshot others.

URL: I own the URL addresses for *Ann Eckhart* in just about every configuration possible (.com, .net, etc.), as well as several other website addresses for my other businesses. Since I have a blog, YouTube channel, and books, it is an integral part of my "branding" strategy to control my web presence.

You can quickly and relatively inexpensively get a personalized

URL from a site such as GoDaddy.com. You can then point that URL directly to your YouTube channel. Or, if you have a blog as I do, you can point your URL there. I direct people to my blog at *AnnEckhart.com*, where they can then find the links for all my social networking sites, including YouTube.

Purchasing dedicated URL addresses and renewing them yearly are just more parts of the branding process. Fortunately, it is an expense you can write-off come tax time.

VIEWS VS. SUBSCRIBERS: Most people start on YouTube focused solely on gaining subscribers. And while the number of subscribers you have is important in your channel's overall growth and your brand, more important is the number of views your videos get.

I have seen people worried about gaining subscribers that they have PAID people to subscribe to their channels. However, just because someone subscribes to your channel does not mean they will watch your videos. You only earn AdSense revenue from people WATCHING your videos, so paying for subscribers is a huge waste of time and money.

Only when someone watches your monetized videos and sees or clicks on the ads that are there will you earn any Google AdSense revenue. To attract viewers, you need to produce quality content. Not all subscribers will watch all your videos, and not all viewers will become subscribers. Suppose you have one of two videos that draw many viewers from internet searches or YouTube promoting them. In that case, you may end up making a lot of AdSense money from people just watching your videos, even if they do not end up subscribing.

However, if you are like me and you are doing YouTube for both profit AND fun, you will be consistently uploading new videos. While I have a handful of videos with current views over 100,000, as of this writing, most of my videos average about 3,000 views each within the first week, some a bit less and some a bit more. Of course, the longer my videos remain on YouTube, the more views they will get. Your videos will continue to earn AdSense money as long as people continue to watch them!

I focus on creating quality content that I am personally interested in, hoping that the viewers will respond. While my videos work in conjunction with my blog to bring in AdSense revenue, I never make a video thinking that it will make me money. I make videos that I enjoy filming and that I hope others will benefit from. Sometimes my favorite videos are the least viewed. However, I just continue making the videos I want to make, and eventually, like-minded people find them.

Making videos is a time-consuming process, so if I am not having fun, I will not do it. Viewers are smart and will see right through an attempt to film videos strictly done for views. Be yourself, have fun, and the views and subscribers will come!

ACCOUNTING & TAXES: Wait a minute, you might be thinking. Taxes?! What do taxes have to do with having a YouTube channel? The title of this book has the word "Profit" in it, and whenever you are earning money, you will have to hand over a part of it to the government.

You must think of your YouTube channel as a business, and businesses bring in profits and have expenses. Keeping track of your expenses will prove valuable at tax time as these business-related purchases count as deductions on your tax bill.

I personally hire an accountant to handle my tax filings for me, but I still must provide him with my documentation and a list of my yearly expenses. Fortunately, YouTube makes it easy to track your AdSense income as Google will mail you out a tax form in January for the previous year's revenue. However, you will also need to track any other income you earn from your channel via sponsorships and affiliate/referral links.

I keep a very basic accounting ledger for my YouTube channel income and expenses. Every month, I record my AdSense earnings and any other money that I made from my channel, such as sponsorship dollars and income earned using my affiliate and referral links. I separate each of these as they are taxed differently. While Google sends me a tax form, I do not always get forms from my other income sources. For instance, while Amazon sends out Amazon Affiliate tax forms, I belong to several other affiliate sites that do not. However, regardless of whether you receive a tax form, you STILL must track all the money you earn from your videos.

After I have recorded my gross YouTube income for the month, I tally up my expenses. Every month I track how much I pay for my:

- Internet
- Cell phone
- Office supplies
- Equipment
- Props
- Postage
- Mileage
- Travel

Note that these are the categories I personally find that I spend money on for my channel; you may not have all of these or add other ones. Regardless of what category your expenses fall into, it is important you record what you are spending on your YouTube channel so that you can deduct those expenses come tax time.

FUN FACTS

Current Top 10 Youtube Marketing Advice Channels:

1. Neil Patel
2. Entrepreneur
3. Google Webmasters
4. Google Analytics
5. Backlinko

6. Dottotech
7. WPBeginner – Word Press Tutorials
8. Ahrefs
9. Lisa Irby
10. HubSpot

CHAPTER SEVEN:

A DAY IN THE LIFE

Being a YouTuber involves more than just filming and uploading videos. In this chapter, I will share a day in my life of everything I do to film, edit, upload, and release YouTube videos, sharing how I film both podcast and vlog-style content.

First up I will walk you through the process for uploading videos to my main channel, which is *The Reselling Report with Ann Eckhart.* I currently upload a new video on this channel every Friday. Since the videos go live at 8 am Central time, I actually film them the day before to give me plenty of time to edit, upload, and do all of the back-end work before scheduling them to go live the following morning. I am certainly not getting up a 6 am to film a weekly news show; after all, I am not trying to compete with *Dateline* or *20/10*

Before I even grab my camera to start recording, I first start the video creation process by going onto my desktop computer and searching for the latest reselling news. I have several retail and e-commerce news sites that I check every week, and I also look at the respective Facebook pages for Ebay, Etsy, and Poshmark to see what, if anything, they may have posted. I then do numerous Google searches to find any other important news to share with my fellow reseller audience.

Once I have all of the websites arranged in order of how I plan to present them during the show, I grab my iPhone to begin filming. *The Reselling Report* functions much like a podcast in that I do not film myself or use video clips; instead, I insert graphics, typically the business logos of the sites I am referencing. **I can produce the videos on my iPhone by opening the iMovie app**, inserting the first graphic I want to use, and then clicking on the **Voiceover** option. I record each segment and then listen back to the entire recording before deciding if it is ready to be uploaded.

Once I am happy with the finished product, **I save the video from the iMovie app to my camera roll at 750HD.** This usually takes a few minutes, depending on the length of the video.

Once the video is saved to my camera roll, I **open the YouTube app on my phone,** make sure I am logged into my *The Reselling Report* channel, and **click on the small video camera icon** at the top of the page to begin the upload process. I then **choose the saved video from my camera roll.** I type one word into both the **title** and **description fields** (you just need to type something into these sections to begin the upload process; I type up the full titles and description boxes on my computer after the videos are uploaded). I make sure that the **privacy setting is turned to "Private"** so that the video does not go live immediately (remember that I schedule my videos for the following day; plus, I need to do some work on the back end before they go live).

I then **click Upload** and wait for the video to be uploaded to my channel. How long this takes depends on the length of the video. For videos over ten minutes, I typically make sure to turn the "sleep" setting on my phone off before uploading. If my phone goes into "sleep" mode during the upload process, the upload will be disrupted, and I will have to start the process all over again.

While the video is uploading, I word on adding the links to the articles I referenced during the show into the *Show Notes* section of my description box. I do this by first copying and pasting each URL into the TinyURL.com website so that the website address is shortened, which gives the list of links a much cleaner look. I then copy and paste the shortened links into my description box text, which I save in a word document.

Once the video has successfully been uploaded, I **switch over to my desktop computer to** take care of the best-handled details on a laptop versus my phone. I log onto YouTube and go into my **YouTube studio**. I then click on the **My Videos icon** on the left-hand side of the page and am taken to my channel videos list. The video that I just uploaded should be the very first video at the top of the page. I hover my mouse over the video, which will bring up several icons. I click on the **pencil icon**, which is called **Details,** to access the **Video details** page.

First, I type in a **keyword loaded title so** that people who are not subscribed to my channel might find it. I also try to make the title sound exciting to encourage people to watch it. There are so many videos on YouTube these days, making it extremely competitive. You must be creative in getting people to click on your videos, especially when they first go live.

After the title, I go into a Word document I have on my computer and copy/paste a block of text that I put into the **description box.** For *The Reselling Report,* the text is as follows:

Visit my Amazon store for all of my books (both under my name and under my Jean Lee Publishing pen name), reselling supplies, and household favorites: https://amzn.to/36p4UwQ

SHOW NOTES: Here, I link all of the articles I referenced during the show. This list changes weekly.

Information on the show is provided under the Fair Use Act. PLEASE be sure to do your own further research on any topics discussed.

Subscribe to my VLOG channel: https://tinyurl.com/yyy5m7xl

Join my FREEBIES & DEALS Facebook group:
https://tinyurl.com/ww5e8t6

Read my BLOG: http://www.anneckhart.com

"Like" my FACEBOOK page: http://www.facebook.com/anneckhart

Follow me on TWITTER: http://www.twitter.com/ann_eckhart

Find me on INSTAGRAM: http://instagram.com/ann_eckhart

I've designed several TEE-SHIRTS & COFFEE MUGS:
https://www.teepublic.com/user/seeannsave

DISCLAIMER: This is not a sponsored video. If disclosed,
some products were sent to me for review. Links
may contain affiliates/referrals.

At the bottom of the description box, I add **three hashtags**, which YouTube will put at the top of the video when it goes live. This is a new YouTube feature, and it works to help people find similar videos through hashtags. I typically include #reselling #ebay #poshmark as my three tags, as these are the most popular in search.

The **Tags** field is at the very bottom of the page. Here is where you can add even more words (think of tags as hashtags without the # symbol) to help potential viewers find your videos when they do a YouTube search. I keep an extensive list of these tag words, separated by commas, in the same Word document that I have my description box information. I can simply copy and paste this block of words into the tags section of every video. Note that the tags I use on my *The Reselling Report* channel are different from those I use on my vlog channel. I then click on the **SAVE** button before moving on to edit another section.

Next, I monetize my video by clicking on the **Monetization icon (the "$" symbol).** Clicking on that dollar icon brings me to the **Video monetization page**. At the top of the page is a **Monetization box**; I select **On** from the drop-down menu. This will then allow me to access the option under the **Type of ads** section of the page. I check every box available to me: **Overlay ads, Sponsored cards, Skippable video ads,** and **Non-skippable video ads**. The Display ads option is automatically selected for you by YouTube.

At the bottom of this page is **Location of video ads**. If my video is over 10 minutes long, I can select all three options: **Before video (pre-roll), During video (mid-roll),** and **After video (post-roll)**. Under the During video (mid-roll) option, click on **MANAGE MID-ROLLS**, which brings up a pop-up window titled **$ AD BREAKS**. Here is where I can choose where the ads that run in the middle of my videos will appear. These ads bring in the most AdSense revenue, so it is essential to make sure you place them strategically. Too many ads can turn viewers off, but not enough can negatively affect your AdSense earnings. I generally like to place ads around the 4-5-minute marks of each of my videos, although for really long videos (over thirty minutes), I will use less so as not to turn off viewers with too many ads.

On the **$ Ad breaks page**, you can click on **+ AD BREAK** to add in however many ads you want to appear. Let's say that the video I am working on is 20 minutes long. I will likely add in 4 ad breaks. I will then move over to the **PLACE AUTOMATICALLY** column to enter in the times of 4, 8, 12, and 16 minutes. Note that you can also manually place the ads using the scrolling template at the bottom of the page, but I personally find it easier to just enter in the times. Once I am done placing my ads, I click on the **CONTINUE** icon to be taken back to the Video monetization page.

After I have typed in my title, copy, pasted my description and tags, and set up my video's monetization, I then go back to the main **Video detail page (the pencil icon titled "Details")**. Until now, I have been using the links on the left side of the page to edit my video's information. Now I will focus on the right side of the page and the options that appear there.

I like to schedule my videos, and I do this under the **Visibility** section. When I upload my video from my iPhone to YouTube, I made sure that it was set to "Private." Now I can change that from **Private to Unlisted, Members Only, Public (set as instant Premiere),** or **Schedule**. I click on the **Schedule** option, which brings up a new window of possibilities. I choose to schedule my video for the following day at 8 am Central time, meaning my video will stay private until YouTube publishes it at that time. I could also choose the **Set as Premiere** option so that my subscribers would see a live countdown before the video goes live. Premiere also features a live chat option where viewers can chat with one another while the video plays. Some creators schedule premieres to be in the chat once the video goes live to talk with their viewers. Premieres are a great way to encourage engagement with your viewers by providing you a way to connect with them directly.

Since I schedule *The Reselling Report* for 8 am Friday mornings, I do not use the Premiere feature as I will still be asleep when the video goes live. I have, however, used the Premiere feature when uploading vlog style videos. Chatting with your viewers when your videos go live does help increase engagement and create more loyal subscribers, so it is something to consider doing, at least from time to time.

Once I have scheduled my video, I click on **DONE,** and the pop-up window collapses. Note that you do not have to schedule your videos to go up at any particular time; you could just make them live once you have added your title and description along with setting up the video's monetization. However, the YouTube algorithm seems to favor channels where the videos go up on set days at set times. And if you like to film videos ahead of time, scheduling them will help keep you organized. Many YouTube creators will film several videos on the same day and schedule them to go live over the following days or even weeks.

The next section you can attend to is **Playlists**. Playlists allow you to set up categories for your videos. For instance, I have playlists for Ebay videos, subscription boxes, vacation vlogs, and shopping hauls. If you are creating different types of videos, even if they are under the same general theme, you may want to consider creating playlists. When someone watches a video in a playlist, it will automatically play the next video in the line-up. Therefore, playlists help keep viewers on your channel and watching your videos.

The next section is the **End Screens**. Here you can add **Elements** to the end of your video that viewers can click on. You can add links to the following: **Video, Playlist, Subscribe, Channel, Link,** and **Merchandise**.

Adding a **Video element** lets you choose from **Most recent up-load, Best for viewer,** or **Choose specific video.** I typically select the "Best for viewer option," but you can decide what is best for each video. For instance, if you referenced another one of your videos in the video you are uploading, you could select that one.

If you have created **Playlists** on your channel, you can also choose to add one of those to your video. **Subscribe** is another option, and, along with "Video" is my favorite option to add. **Channel** allows you to add another channel; I use it to promote my own second channel. **Link** lets you add a clickable link to a URL that takes the viewer off of YouTube and to another site. And finally, **Merchandise** will take viewers to items you have created using the TeeSpring design feature that YouTube offers to channels with 10,000 or more subscribers. I have created merchandise using YouTube's TeeSpring feature as well as on the off-site platform TeePublic.

I typically only choose the "Video" and "Subscribe" elements for my videos; getting viewers to watch another video on my channel and having them subscribe are the two most important things I would like them to do. You want to be careful of loading too many end screen elements as your screen will look too cluttered to viewers, and they likely will not choose any of the options available.

The last box you can open is **Cards,** which, according to You-Tube, "are designed to complement videos and enhance the viewer experience with relevant info." Cards help to point viewers to your other videos and off-YouTube content. You have four different types of **Cards** to choose from: **Video, Playlist, Channel,** and **Link**.

Video cards allow you to link to another public YouTube video that viewers might be interested in. **Playlist cards** let you connect to another public YouTube playlist. **Channel cards** will enable you to link to a channel that you want to direct viewers to do; for example, maybe you are doing a collaboration video with another creator, so you create a "Channel card" to link them directly. And finally, **Link cards** allow you to link to **Associate website cards**, **Crowdfunding cards**, and **Merchandise cards**.

I personally do not use the "Card" options, feeling that the "End screen" options provide the same benefits. However, as you continue with your YouTube journey, you can take time to play around with the "Card" features to see if they world for you.

My title, description, tags, monetization, schedule, playlist, and end screen options are all finished. I am now ready to tackle the final task before my video is ready to launch: the **thumbnail**. A YouTube thumbnail is the image that appears next to the title of your video. It is the first thing a potential viewer sees, and it is imperative to help get people to click on your video and watch it.

You can use several design apps and programs to create correctly sized YouTube thumbnails. I personally use **Thumbnail Maker**, which is available from Google. YouTube thumbnails need to be 1280x720 pixels; be uploaded in JPG, GIF, or PNG format; and remain under the 2MB limit.

To create my thumbnails, I first select a graphic or graphics that I want to use. Sometimes I will use a photo, other times graphics, and in some cases, I will use both. Using an app such as Thumbnail Maker makes it extremely easy to create my thumbnails right on my phone. And once I save the finished product, I can either email it to myself to add to my video on my desktop; or I can simply use the **YouTube studio app** on my phone to upload it directly.

I also have a vlog channel, *Ann Eckhart Vlogs*; but the process of uploading videos to that channel is relatively the same as for the *The Reselling Report* channel. The only difference is in the filming. While I focus on photos and voiceovers for my reselling news show, when I am filming a vlog, I am either filming myself or the events around me.

When filming video clips using my phone, I make sure to hold it horizontally, not vertically. Filming on an iPhone held vertically will result in black bars appearing on either side of your footage. Filming horizontally makes it so that your footage takes up the entire screen. When I am vlogging, I simply film my various video clips, which are automatically saved to my phone's camera. When I am ready to put all of the clips together, I do the same as I did for uploading my *The Reselling Report* video using my iPhone:

- I put all the clips together in iMovie,
- I save the finished video to my camera roll at 750HD
- If the video is over 10 minutes, I make sure to turn the sleep mode off on my phone so as my camera will not switch off during the uploading process
- I open the YouTube app and click on the little camera icon
- I choose the video from my camera roll
- I type one word into the title and description field and make sure the video is set to private
- I then click upload

- Once the video is uploaded, I switch over to my computer
- I add in my title, fill out the description box, add in my three leading hashtags, copy/paste my list of tags, monetize the video, choose a playlist, add my end cards, and finally schedule the for the time and date I want it to go live

Once my videos go live, I then share them out to my social media accounts. I use the "Share" icons located underneath my videos to post them to my Facebook page, Twitter account, and Pinterest board. I also put up a post on Instagram, both on my page's feed as well as in my "stories". Since I have over 10,000 Instagram followers, I am able to add the "swipe up" feature to my stories, allowing followers to go straight to my video from Instagram. And finally, I post the video to my blog so that readers who are subscribed will get an email letting them know that a new video is now up.

FUN FACTS

Top YouTube Controversies In 2020:

1. ImJayStation faking his girlfriend's death for subs
2. Shane Dawson's rise and fall
3. Myka Stauffer rehoming her adopted son
4. Miranda Sings exposed for past racist remarks
5. Jenna Marbles quitting the site
6. Drama in the beauty community between James Charles, Jeffree Starr, and Tati Westbrook
7. YouTube stars having parties despite the COVID-19 pandemic
8. Jake Paul involved in looting during the George Floyd protests
9. Pewdiepie
10. Brie Larson starting a channel

CHAPTER EIGHT:

THE BIG LIST OF YOUTUBE TAGS

I f you watch enough YouTube videos, you will likely or have already come across "tag" videos. "Tags" are simply quizzes or questionnaires that YouTube creators answer on camera. Think back to your school days when you answered quizzes printed in magazines, either alone or with a group of your friends. It is the same concept as it was before the internet, except now it is done on camera for anyone to view!

Whether you are looking to start a YouTube channel or already have one, filming "tag" videos is a fun and easy way to create content for your channel and engage with your audience. You do not need a fancy set up – you simply sit in front of the camera, read off the questions, and answer them honestly. "Tags" are some of the most uncomplicated videos to film, so they are a great way to get started on your YouTube journey or to add new videos to your existing channel without having to do the work of thinking up an original topic of your own.

"Tags" have been around since the beginning of YouTube and are extremely popular. If you are struggling to figure out ideas for videos, you will want to give "tags" a try as they provide you with an already proven concept and format. And by using the "tags" in this book, which have already been proven to attract viewers, you'll increase your chance of your video being found by people who are watching or searching for "tag" videos.

Some things to remember when going through the "tags" listed in this book:

Order: I have arranged the" tags" in this book in alphabetical order, not in the order of popularity.

History: Note that YouTube started gaining popularity with young girls and women doing makeup related videos, so many of the "tags" in this book have their origins in the beauty community. They also tend to skew to a younger audience (many tags have school-related questions). However...

Feel Free to Edit: Neither the" tag" questions nor the "tags" themselves are written in stone. Feel free to add questions or to omit questions you are uncomfortable answering. If you like the general theme of a "tag" but do not feel the questions really relate to you, change them up. And only do the "tags" that genuinely appeal to you. Viewers want to watch FUN "tag" videos, not videos where the person is bored or struggling to answer the questions. Make sure you look over the questions first before sitting down to film, so you are prepared and are not left stumbling to answer them.

Tag Others: A great way to network on Facebook is to "tag" other YouTubers in your own "tag" videos. After you have finished answering the "tag" questions, end your video by mentioning a couple of other channels where you'd like to see the "tag" done. Let those channel creators know you have tagged them (you can message other YouTube creators through YouTube or on social media). Even better is to "tag" ALL of your viewers; ending your video by saying, "I now tag all of YOU to do this video, and be sure to let me know if you do it!" encourages your viewers to engage with you actively, which creates viewer loyalty and helps to grow your channel.

Best Practices: A general rule of thumb is to put the "tag" questions in the description bar of your video so that others can use your list to answer the questions themselves. If you are doing a "tag," you saw on someone else's channel, be sure to mention them. Not only is it a great way to network with fellow YouTubers, but you also do not want your audience to think you came up with a "tag" on your own when in fact, it has been used by many other creators before you.

If you are new to YouTube, you will be limited to uploading videos no longer than 10 minutes; so, keep that in mind as you are filming "tags" with a long list of questions. Even if you have been upgraded to being able to upload videos over 10 minutes long, YouTube viewers tend to prefer videos no longer than 15 minutes.

Create Your Own: As I mentioned, these "tags" are open to editing and revamping. And of course, nothing is stopping you from creating your own unique "tags"! In fact, YouTube could undoubtedly use some fresh, new "tags,"; so, do not hesitate to make up some new ones of your own!

"Tags" are fun, easy to film, popular, and encourage engagement – add some "tag" videos to your channel and see how they not only boost your content but also drive viewers to your channel!

THE ACCENT TAG: Different products and activities are called different things in different countries (for instance, we say "sweatshirts" in America, but the British call them "jumpers"). In this tag, figure out the item or action each question is referring to and share what you call it in your country!

1. What is it called when you throw toilet paper at a house?
2. What is the bug that when you touch it, it curls into a ball?
3. What is the bubbly carbonated drink called?

4. What do you call gym shoes?
5. What do you say to address a group of people?
6. What do you call the kind of spider (or spider-like creature) that has an oval-shaped body and extremely long legs?
7. What do you call your grandparents?
8. What do you call the wheeled contraption in which you carry groceries at the supermarket?
9. What do you call it when rain falls while the sun is shining?
10. What is the thing you change the TV channel with?

THE AUSTRALIAN TAG: This tag is for the Aussies to answer! If you are not from Australia but have traveled there, you can undoubtedly alter a few of the questions to relate to your time Down Under!

1. Which state do you live in?
2. What states have you visited around Australia?
3. What do you order at Boost Juice?
4. Golden Gaytimes or Pavlovas?
5. Cricket or AFL?
6. Who is your favorite Australian actor/actress?
7. Describe your formal night in high school?
8. Do you like vegemite? How do you like to eat it?
9. Have you ever seen or petted a kangaroo?
10. Have you ever seen the Sydney Harbour Bridge?
11. Do you say...Mate? G'day? Jumper or sweater?
12. Overall, what do you think of Australia?

THE BABY TAG: If you have a little one, you will have fun answering these questions! Not only will it make for a great memory to have on film, but it will also help you connect with other parents. Note that you can answer these questions regardless of your child's age as other moms and dads are always looking for advice.

1. Your baby's weight and height at birth? At two months?
2. How many newborn diapers did your baby go through? Size 1's? What brand?
3. How long was your baby in newborn clothes? In 0-3 month clothes?
4. What size diaper bag? What brand?
5. Did your baby use a baby swing?
6. Would you recommend buying a playmat?
7. Would you recommend buying a bouncy seat?
8. Would you recommend buying a bassinet or a pack-n-play
9. Did your child use a soother/pacifier, and what brand?
10. One must-have item for your baby?
11. The item you would not have bought?
12. Any advice for breastfeeding or bottle feeding?
13. What works/worked to calm your baby down?
14. What is/was your bedtime routine
15. Your hair and eye color, your partner's, and the baby's?
16. Any last advice for new parents?

BAND MUSIC TAG: This is the first of several music-themed tags in this book. If you love music, these sorts of tags are not only fun to do, but they can also help you connect with viewers and other YouTube creators who share your taste in music!

1. Shuffle your playlist and tell us the first ten songs that show up.
2. How many bands have you seen live?

3. Which was the best band you have seen live?
4. Which was the worst band you have seen live?
5. Have you ever met someone in a band?
6. Have you ever been in a band yourself?
7. Can you play any instruments?
8. Which band would you give anything to see?
9. Do you have any concert tee shirts or other clothing?
10. Favorite song this minute?
11. What is your favorite genre of music?
12. What song has the highest play count on your playlist?
13. What song would you choose to sing karaoke?
14. What song should never be sung publicly unless by a professional?
15. What is your favorite album?
16. What would be the best line up for a concert festival?
17. Do you subscribe to any music magazines?
18. Kiss, marry or avoid the first three artists that show up when you shuffle your playlist.
19. Do you have any music posters up in your room?
20. Do you have the same musical tastes as your friends?
21. Have you seen any musicals?
22. If you could see any musical, what would you see?
23. Do you listen to the radio?
24. What is the worst song ever released?
25. Are you listening to any music right now?
26. What was the last song you heard?
27. What is the next concert you are going to?

BEST FRIEND TAG #1: Grab your best buddy and film this video side-by-side. Or, if you both have YouTube channels, you can each film this tag where you answer the questions alone or by interviewing one another and then encourage your viewers to check out your friend's channel for their answers!

1. How and when did you meet?
2. What were your first impressions of each other?
3. What is your favorite memory of something you have done together?
4. Describe each other in one word?
5. What is one thing that annoys you about the other person?
6. What is one thing you each love about the other person?
7. If you could go anywhere in the world together, where would it be?
8. Favorite inside joke?
9. Who takes longer to get ready in the morning?
10. What's the other person's eye color – do not cheat!

BEST FRIEND TAG #2: Here is another version of a best friend tag. This fun video is to be filmed alongside your best friend and can be done in two different ways. One is for each of you to give your own answers to the questions, or you can quiz each other. If you both have YouTube channels, have each of you film a video asking the other one the questions and then cross-promote your videos to draw traffic to both of your channels!

1. Middle name?
2. Mom's maiden name?
3. Favorite sport?
4. Favorite season?
5. Favorite holiday?
6. Favorite film?
7. Favorite ice cream flavor?
8. What three things do you (or your friend) always carry with you?
9. What are three things always in your (or your friend's) fridge?

10. If you (or your friend) were stranded on a deserted island, what are three things you (or your friend) could not live without besides food, water, and loved ones?

11. Favorite three songs of all time?

12. Shoe size?

13. If you (or your friend) won a contest and the grand prize was the services of either a cook or housekeeper, which would you (or your friend) choose?

14. Prefer movies or television?

15. Hot chocolate, coffee, or tea?

16. Chocolate or non-chocolate candy?

17. Favorite teacher (or boss if you are older and work a job)?

18. Two favorite and two least favorite classmates or co-workers?

19. If you (or your friend) were eating lunch in a restaurant and the food was inedible, would you (or your friend): a. Send it back; b. eat it and not say anything to anyone; c. not eat it and if the server asks, tell the truth; or d. not eat it and if asked, lie and say it was fine.

20. If someone talked loudly during a movie, would you (or your friend): a. Shush them very loudly; b. move to another section of the theatre; or c. inform the manager?

21. If you (or your friend) won the lottery, what would you (or your friend) buy first?

BOOK TAG: If you love to read, then the Book Tag is for you! There is an active community of readers and book reviewers on YouTube, so this tag can help you connect with other book worms out there!

1. Do you have a particular place at home to read?

2. Do you use a bookmark or a random piece of paper to mark your page?
3. Can you stop reading anytime you want, or do you have to stop at a particular page, chapter, part, etc.?
4. Do you eat or drink while reading?
5. Can you read while listening to music or watching TV?
6. One book at a time or several at once?
7. Do you only read at home or everywhere you go?
8. Do you read aloud or silently in your head?
9. Do you read ahead or skip pages?
10. Do you like breaking the spine or keeping it new?
11. Do you write in books?
12. What is your favorite book of all time?
13. Who is your favorite author of all time?
14. What are you currently reading?

THE BOYFRIEND TAG: This tag is meant to be done on camera with your boyfriend, with you asking him the questions! Note that this is a rather long tag, so you may want to edit some of the questions or break it into two parts. If you are married, note that there is a "Husband Tag" later in this chapter.

1. Where did we meet?
2. Where was our first date?
3. What was your first impression of me?
4. When did you meet my family?
5. Do I have any weird obsessions?
6. How long have we been together?
7. Do we have any traditions?
8. What was our first road trip?
9. What was the first thing you noticed about me?
10. What is my favorite restaurant?
11. What do we argue about the most?
12. Who wears the pants in our relationship?

13. What is my favorite TV show?
14. What is one food that I do not like?
15. What drink do I order when we go out to eat?
16. What shoe size do I wear?
17. What is my favorite kind of sandwich?
18. What is one talent I have?
19. What would I eat every day if I could?
20. What is my favorite cereal?
21. What is my favorite music?
22. What is my favorite sports team?
23. What is my eye color?
24. Who is my best friend?
25. What is something you do that I wish you did not?
26. Where am I from?
27. What kind of cake would you bake me on my birthday?
28. Do I play any sports?
29. What can I spend hours doing?
30. If I could live anywhere, where would it be?

CHILD-FREE TAG: While it may feel like the only older women on YouTube are all moms, there are plenty of content creators who do not have kids. If you are one of them and are continually being asked about having children, this is a great tag to do to answer your critics!

1. Do you like or dislike children?
2. Why did you opt-out of parenthood?
3. Do you think your childhood experiences and/or parents' actions influenced your decision not to have children?
4. What is the most common reaction/comment you get when people find out you are child-free?
5. Do you have any child-free friends or relatives?

6. Do you think people are aware that parenthood is a choice?
7. How do you feel/react when your loved ones announce they are expecting?
8. Are you worried one day you might regret your decision?
9. For women, don't you want to experience being pregnant?
10. Is your current partner child-free as well?
11. Is it possible to be in a happy, fulfilling relationship without children?
12. Define parenthood in one word.
13. Do you think you would be a good parent?
14. Do you have pets? If so, do you think you are transferring the nurturing and love intended for a child on to your pets?
15. Which child-free stereotype do you not fit?
16. Is it hard to find a child-free partner?
17. Which label do you prefer: child-free or childless?
18. Do you actively encourage the people around you to think about their reproductive choices?
19. Are you worried about who will take care of you when you are old?
20. What is the best part about being child-free?

THE CHRISTMAS TAG: Do this tag after Thanksgiving or early December as a fun lead up to the holidays!

1. What is your favorite Christmas movie?
2. What is your favorite Christmas color combination, green and red or silver and gold?
3. Do you like to stay in your pajamas or dress up on Christmas Day?
4. If you could only buy one person a present this year,

who would it be?

5. Do you open your presents on Christmas Eve or Christmas morning?
6. Have you ever built a gingerbread house?
7. What do you like to do during Christmas vacation?
8. Any Christmas wishes?
9. Favorite Christmas smell?
10. Favorite Christmas meal?
11. Favorite Christmas dessert or candy?

THE CLOSET CONFIDENTIAL TAG: If you love clothing, shoes, and accessories, this is the tag for you! This tag is even more fun if you show the pieces you reference, so read over the questions first and pull out the items you want to show your viewers.

1. What is the oldest item in your wardrobe/closet?
2. What is the newest item in your closet?
3. What is the most expensive item in your closet?
4. What is the most affordable/cheapest item in your closet that you use the most?
5. What was your biggest clothing bargain?
6. What clothing item was the biggest waste of money?
7. What are your current three favorite clothing items?
8. What is the most outrageous item in your closet right now?
9. What is your favorite piece of clothing that you have gotten as a gift?
10. What is your most comfortable piece of clothing?
11. What is the most uncomfortable clothing item you own, but you love it because of how it makes you look?
12. Show us your favorite, complete outfit, including shoes and accessories.
13. Show us your favorite black and favorite white items?

14. At what store do you buy most of your clothing?

THE DAD TAG: Grab your dad for this sit-down question and answer session! Look for the "Mom Tag" later in this chapter.

1. What was I like as a child?
2. What do you think of my making YouTube videos?
3. What is something funny I did when I was younger?
4. Have you learned anything from my videos?
5. What is a weird habit of mine?
6. If you had to rename me, what would my name be?
7. When we go out to eat, what do I order?
8. What is the one thing you wish I would do?
9. What is something I do that annoys you?
10. What is something I obsess over?
11. Where would you like to see me in 10 years?
12. When were you the proudest of me?
13. What is the worst thing I have ever done?
14. What is your favorite moment of us together?
15. How was I in school?
16. What would you change if you could raise me again?
17. Describe my perfect mate?

DIRTY SECRETS TAG: This tag sounds naughty, but the questions are, for the most part, innocent! If you feel uncomfortable answering any of these questions, do not hesitate to leave them out.

1. What was your first cuss word?
2. What was your first R-rated movie?
3. Who was your first kiss?
4. What do you wear to bed?
5. Have you ever caught your parents in the act?

6. Have you ever cheated in a relationship?
7. What kinds of underwear do you wear?
8. Have you ever pooped your pants?
9. Have you ever had a fantasy dream about a celebrity?
10. What is your favorite feature on your crush or significant other?

THE DISNEY TAG: If you love all things Disney, this is the tag for you! Disney fanatics are a big community on YouTube, so this tag is a great way to connect with others who share your love of the Mouse.

1. A scene in any Disney movie you wish you could experience?
2. Have you ever been to any Disney theme parks?
3. When was the first time you went to a Disney Park?
4. An unforgettable experience/moment you have had at the Disney Parks?
5. What non-Disney song(s) reminds you or brings back memories of Disney and/or the Parks?
6. If you could choose any of the characters to be your best friend, who would you choose?
7. Who are your favorite Disney princesses?
8. Name a scene/moment in any Disney movie that never fails to make you cry?
9. What is the first Disney movie you remember seeing?
10. What is your favorite Disney movie?
11. What is your favorite Disney song?
12. Have you ever taken a Disney Cruise?

THE DREAM TAG: The Dream Tag is great for both guys and gals of any age, making it one of the most popular tags for all YouTubers to film!

1. Do you dream?
2. What did you dream about last night?
3. How many dreams do you usually remember?
4. Do you have a dream journal?
5. How often do you have nightmares?
6. Do you lucid dream?
7. Do you dream in color?
8. Do you dream in the first person?
9. Do you have recurring dreams?
10. Have you ever had déjà vu after a dream?

THE 80'S TAG: If you were a child, teen, or young adult during the 1980s, this a fun tag to film!

1. What was your age range in the '80s?
2. Favorite 80's movie?
3. Favorite 80's cartoon?
4. Favorite 80's TV show?
5. Favorite thing about the '80s?
6. Where did you live in 1985?
7. Favorite 80's cereal?
8. Favorite 80's candy?
9. Favorite 80's song?
10. Favorite 80's artist?
11. Favorite 80's fashion trend?
12. Your favorite pastime in the '80s?

8 "HAVE YOU EVER" QUESTIONS TAG: This tag was first intro-duced as part of a series of tags counting down from 10 to one; I have one through five together in this book as you can easily film one video to cover all five. However, I have divided five to

10 up alphabetically as they have enough questions in each to make up their own videos.

1. Have you ever liked someone who had a girlfriend/ boyfriend?
2. Have you ever had your heart broken?
3. Have you ever been out of the country?
4. Have you ever done something outrageously dumb?
5. Have you ever been back-stabbed by a friend?
6. Have you ever had sex on the beach?
7. Have you ever dated someone younger than you?
8. Have you ever read an entire book in one day?

50 RANDOM FACTS ABOUT ME TAG: Film a video stating 50 random facts about yourself! Sounds easy, but most people stumble unless they write out the 50 things beforehand!

50 THINGS NEAR ME TAG: Make sure you are filming in a room with lots of stuff in it so that you can quickly grab and show 50 items that are close to where you are sitting! A desk, makeup area, kitchen, or bathroom all work well for this tag as you will have lots of items within easy reach.

15 QUESTIONS TAG: There are many these numbered, general-themed tags to choose from, making them great for YouTubers of all ages!

1. What do you think you can do well but really cannot?
2. What is a difficult word for you to pronounce?
3. What is a favorite TV show from your childhood?
4. What are your virtues and your vices?

5. What is more important: love, fame, power, or money?
6. If you could live in any era/time period, when would it be and why?
7. If you had to redo your entire wardrobe with clothing from only two stores, what would those stores be, and why?
8. Can you recall what you were doing a year ago on this day?
9. Do you have reoccurring dreams?
10. What is your horoscope sign?
11. What does your dream bedroom look like?
12. What position do you sleep in?
13. Who is your favorite vampire of all time?
14. What are you currently wearing on your feet?
15. Do you have neat handwriting? Show us!

GET TO KNOW ME TAG: The "Get to Know Me Tag" is a great video to film for new YouTubers as it offers an easy way for you to introduce yourself to your audience! However, even if you have been making videos for a while, it is still worth doing for your subscribers to understand you better.

1. What is your name?
2. Any nicknames?
3. When is your birthday?
4. In what city/state/country were you born?
5. What is your zodiac/star sign?
6. What is your natural hair color?
7. How long is your hair?
8. What color are your eyes?
9. What are your best physical features?
10. Ever wore, or do you currently wear braces?

11. Do you have any piercings?

12. Do you have any tattoos?

13. Are you right-handed or left-handed?

14. Who was your first best friend?

15. What was the first concert you ever attended?

16. What is your favorite movie?

17. What is your favorite television show?

18. What is your favorite color?

19. What is your favorite song?

20. What is your favorite restaurant?

21. What is your favorite store?

22. What is your favorite book?

23. What is your favorite magazine?

24. What is your current mood?

25. Are you single or taken?

26. Do you have, or do you want children?

27. Are you or do you want to be married someday?

28. What is your current career?

29. Do you believe in God?

30. Do you believe in miracles?

31. Do you believe in love at first sight?

32. Do you believe in ghosts and/or aliens?

33. Do you believe in kissing on the first date?

34. Do you believe in yourself?

15 WEIRD QUESTIONS TAG: Most of these questions are not actually that weird, but this is still a fun and easy tag video to film for all ages!

1. What is a nickname only your family calls you?

2. What is one of your weird habits?

3. Do you have any weird phobias?

4. What is a song you secretly love to blast and belt out when you are alone?

5. What is one of your biggest pet peeves?
6. What is one of your nervous habits?
7. What side of the bed do you sleep on?
8. What was the name of your first stuffed animal, and do you still have it today?
9. What is the drink you always order at Starbucks?
10. What is a beauty rule you preach but never actually practice?
11. Which way do you face in the shower?
12. Do you have any weird skills?
13. What is your favorite comfort food?
14. What is a phrase you always say?
15. What do you wear to bed?

FIVE-TO-ONE TAG: I referenced this tag earlier; it was initially a ten-to-one tag, but the length was ridiculous. YouTube likes videos under 15 minutes, so I broke six through ten down into individual tags but left one through five in a single tag format.

Five "Do"

1. Do you think anyone likes you?
2. Do you ever wish you were someone else?
3. Do you know the muffin man?
4. Does the future scare you?
5. Does your family know you have a YouTube channel?

Four "Why"

1. Why are you best friends with your best friend?
2. Why did you get into YouTube?
3. Why did your parents give you the name you have?
4. Why are you doing this tag?

Three "If"

1. If you could have one superpower, what would it be?

2. If you could go back in time and change one thing, what would it be?
3. If you were stranded on a deserted island and could only bring one thing, what would it be?

Two "Would You Ever"

1. Would you ever get back together with any of your ex's if they asked you?
2. Would you ever shave your head to save someone you love?

One Last Question

1. Are you happy with your life now?

40 BEAUTY QUESTIONS TAG: As I mentioned in the introduction to this book, YouTube first became popular with young women making beauty videos. So, many tags such as this one in this book relate to makeup, cosmetics, skincare, and hair!

2. How many times do you wash your face daily?
3. What skin type do you have?
4. What is your current facial wash?
5. Do you exfoliate?
6. What brand of skincare is your favorite?
7. What moisturizer do you use?
8. Do you have freckles?
9. Do you use eye cream?
10. Do you or did you have acne-prone skin?
11. Did you ever have to use Proactive?
12. What foundation do you use?
13. What concealer do you use?
14. Do you know your undertone color?
15. What do you think about fake eyelashes?
16. Did you know that you are supposed to change your

mascara every three months?

17. What brand of mascara do you use?
18. Sephora or MAC or Ulta?
19. Do you have a beauty store card (Sephora, Ulta, MAC, The Body Shop)?
20. What makeup tools do you use?
21. Do you use makeup base or primer for your eyes?
22. Do you use makeup base or primer for your face?
23. What is your favorite eye shadow brand and color?
24. Do you use a pencil or liquid eyeliner?
25. How often do you poke your eyes with an eyeliner pencil?
26. Do you use mineral makeup?
27. What is your favorite lipstick?
28. What is your favorite blush to use?
29. Do you buy any makeup on Ebay?
30. Do you like drugstore makeup?
31. Do you shop at cosmetic outlet stores?
32. Did you ever consider taking a makeup class?
33. Are you clumsy in putting on makeup?
34. Name a makeup crime that you hate.
35. Do you like colorful or neutral shades of makeup?
36. Which celebrity always has great makeup?
37. If you could leave the house using just one makeup item, what would it be?
38. Could you ever leave the house without any makeup on?
39. In your opinion, what is the best makeup line?
40. What do you think of makeup overall?

THE FUN QUESTIONS TAG: Here is another easy tag video to film that will help your audience get to know you!

1. When is your birthday?

2. What are 3 of your favorite colors?
3. What are your three favorite quotes?
4. Are you addicted to YouTube?
5. What are 3 of your favorite shows on TV or YouTube, or both?
6. What are the three qualities you like in a best friend?
7. Do you like your name?
8. If you had the choice to pick your own name, what would it be?
9. What is your fantasy dream?
10. Do you wear makeup?
11. If you could write a book, what would the title be, and what would it be about?
12. What makes you cry?
13. What makes you angry?
14. What makes you happy?
15. What is "fangirling"?
16. What are your three favorite snacks?
17. What are your three favorite foods?
18. What are your three favorite drinks?
19. What are ten random facts about you?
20. What are three fun things you like to do?

FURRY FRIEND TAG: If you have a cat, dog, or other pet, here is a tag just for them!

1. What is your pet's name?
2. What kind of pet is it, and what breed?
3. How long have you had your furry friend?
4. How did you get your pet?
5. How old is your pet?
6. What are some quirky things about your pet's personality?
7. What does your relationship with your pet mean to

you?

8. What are some of your favorite pastimes with your pet?

9. What nicknames do you call your pet?

HAPPY NEW YEAR TAG: This tag video is meant to be filmed close to the New Year; about a week before January 1st is a good time to upload this one!

1. What do you plan to do for New Year's Eve?
2. Do you have any New Year's traditions?
3. Is there anything you love/hate about New Year's family get-togethers?
4. What was your resolution for the past year? Did you complete it?
5. What is your resolution for the upcoming year?
6. What was your favorite thing that happened this past year?
7. What are you most excited about for the coming year?
8. What are three things you would like to accomplish in the next year?
9. What is your favorite thing to eat for New Year's?

HARRY POTTER TAG: Are you a Harry Potter fan? Then this is one tag you will want to do!

1. Favorite Harry Potter book?
2. Favorite Harry Potter movie?
3. Least favorite Harry Potter book?
4. Parts of the books/movies that made you cry?
5. If you could hook up with any Harry Potter character,

who would it be?

6. Favorite character?
7. What would your Patronus be?
8. If you could have the Resurrection Stone, Invisibility Cloak, or the Elder Wand, which would you choose?
9. What House would you be in?
10. If you could meet any member of the cast, who would it be?
11. Have you played any of the Harry Potter video games?
12. If you were on the Quidditch team, which position would you play?
13. Were you happy with the way the series ended?
14. How much does Harry Potter mean to you?

HOLIDAY TAG #1: There are several holidays and time-of-year tags in this book, many with overlapping questions. However, most have enough differences that your audience will not notice if you do them all (if you space them out a bit)!

1. Which holiday or holidays do you celebrate in December?
2. What are you doing for the holidays this year?
3. What is your favorite holiday drink?
4. Candy canes or gingerbread men?
5. What is your favorite holiday song?
6. What is the weirdest holiday gift you have ever received?
7. Have you ever made a snowman?
8. What is your favorite winter fragrance?
9. What is at the top of your wish list this year?
10. What is the most important part of the holidays for you?

HOLIDAY TAG #2: This tag is like the last tag, so I would pick which of the two you like best and simply title it "Holiday Tag," leaving off the number so as not to confuse your audience! Or choose the questions you like best from each to make your own customized tag!

1. What is your favorite holiday movie?
2. Do you like to stay in your PJ's or dress up for the holidays?
3. If you could only buy one person a present this year, who would it be?
4. Have you ever built a gingerbread house?
5. What do you like to do on your holiday break?
6. Favorite holiday smell?
7. Favorite holiday meal or treat?
8. What is your favorite gift you purchased for someone ELSE this year?
9. What is the number one item on your wish list this year?

HUSBAND TAG: Grab your hubby for an on-camera interrogation, err, interview! This tag is meant to be done interview style, not with both people answering the questions. Turn the tables by doing the "Wife Tag," which you will find later in this chapter!

1. Where did we meet?
2. Where was our first date?
3. What was your first impression of me?
4. When did you meet my family?
5. What is one of my weird habits?
6. How long have we been together?
7. Do we have any traditions?
8. What was our first road trip?

9. First thing you noticed about me?
10. What pisses you off the most?
11. Favorite feature about me?
12. Three things I am good at and three things I am not good at?
13. What do we argue about the most?
14. Do I have PMS?
15. Who wears the pants in the relationship?
16. Do I have any weird obsessions?
17. Your nickname for me?
18. What is my favorite restaurant?
19. If I am watching TV, what am I watching?
20. What is one food I do not like?
21. What drink do I order when we go out to eat?
22. What size of shoe do I wear?
23. My favorite sandwich?
24. What is one talent I have?
25. What would I eat every day if I could?
26. My favorite cereal?
27. My favorite kind of music?
28. My favorite sports team?
29. What is my eye color?
30. Who is my best friend?
31. Something you do that I wish you did not do?
32. Where am I from?
33. What kind of cake would you bake me on my birthday?
34. Do I play any sports?
35. What can I spend hours doing?

❖ ❖ ❖

I LOVE FALL TAG: The beauty questions in this tag cause it to appeal mainly to girly girls. However, do not be afraid to omit some of the questions and add others of your own!

1. Favorite Fall lip product?
2. Favorite Fall nail polish?
3. Favorite Fall Starbucks drink?
4. Favorite Fall candle scent?
5. Favorite Fall fashion accessory?
6. Haunted house, hayride, or corn maze?
7. Favorite Halloween movie?
8. Favorite candy to eat on Halloween?
9. What are you dressing up as for Halloween?
10. What is your favorite thing about Fall?

I LOVE SLEEP TAG: If you love a good nap, this tag is right up your alley! Filming this in your pajamas and in your bedroom will give this video great ambiance, too!

1. What is your routine before going to sleep?
2. What do you do when you cannot sleep?
3. What is your favorite sleeping position?
4. What can I wake you up for?
5. At what time does your alarm clock go off?
6. Snooze or get up instantly?
7. Do you sleep in on the weekends?
8. What kind of weird stuff do you do while you are asleep?
9. How many pillows do you have?
10. What do you wear for bed?
11. Do you sleep with or without socks?
12. What size/how big is your bed?
13. The first thing I do when I wake up in the morning is....?
14. Do you dream every night?
15. What dream or nightmare can you remember?
16. What time do you go to bed?
17. How many times do you awaken/get up during the

night?

INSTAGRAM TAG: This tag works best if you have your Instagram page up on your phone or tablet so that you can show the pictures you reference to your viewers. Do not forget to link your Instagram account in your description bar so that your subscribers can follow you there, too!

1. What is your username?
2. When did you create your Instagram account?
3. What is the first picture you posted?
4. How many times do you log in per day and per week?
5. What is your worst picture?
6. Which picture has the most likes?
7. How many followers do you have?
8. How many people are you following?
9. Who is the last person who liked one of your pictures?
10. Name one brand or celebrity you are following?
11. Do any brands or celebrities follow you?
12. Show us your top 3 pictures.
13. What is the last picture on your Instagram feed?

INVADE MY PRIVACY TAG: This tag is filled with many personal, relationship-based questions, so be sure you are comfortable answering them all before you start filming! It is also very long, so consider cutting out the questions you do not want to answer and only focus on those you do to save time.

1. Did you wake up cranky?
2. Would you date an 18-year-old at your current age?
3. Do you prefer to be friends with girls or boys?
4. Would you ever smile at a stranger?
5. Can you commit to one person?

6. How do you look right now?
7. What exactly are you wearing right now?
8. How often do you listen to music?
9. Do you wear jeans or sweats more?
10. Do you think your life will change dramatically before the end of next year?
11. Are you a social or an antisocial person?
12. If the person you like said they liked someone else, what would you say?
13. Are you good at hiding your feelings?
14. Can you drive a stick shift?
15. Do you care if people talk badly about you?
16. Are you going out of town soon?
17. When was the last time you cried?
18. Have you ever liked someone you did not expect to?
19. If you could change your eye color, would you?
20. Name something you must do tomorrow?
21. Name something you dislike about the day you are having?
22. Have you ever liked one of your best friends of the opposite sex?
23. Are you nice to everyone?
24. What are you sitting on right now?
25. Do you think you can last in a relationship for six months and not cheat?
26. Have you ever wanted someone you could not have?
27. Who was the last person you talked to before you went to bed last night?
28. Do you get a lot of colds?
29. Have your pants ever fallen in public?
30. Does anyone hate you?
31. Do you have someone of the opposite sex you can tell everything to?
32. Do you like watching scary movies?
33. Are you a jealous person?
34. If you had to delete one year of your life completely,

which would it be?

35. Did you have a dream last night?
36. Is there anyone you can tell everything to?
37. Do you think you will be married in 5 years?
38. Do you think someone has feelings for you?
39. Do you think someone is thinking about you right now?
40. Did you have a good day yesterday?
41. Were you in a relationship two months ago?
42. If your life anything like it was two years ago?
43. If the person you wish to be with were with you, what would you be doing right now?
44. What is (or was) the best part of school?
45. Do you (or did you) pass notes in school?
46. Do you replay things that have happened over and over in your head?
47. Were you single last summer?
48. What are you supposed to be doing right now?
49. Do not tell me lies: is the last person you texted attractive?

LYRICS TAG: Answer all the following questions with lyrics from songs performed by ONE band or artist. For instance, only answer with lyrics from Elvis songs; i.e., you could answer the question, "Tell us the story of your life" with "I ain't nothin' but a hound dog!" This is a tough tag and one you will want to figure out the answers to before you start filming. If you find it too hard, try answering the questions with any song lyrics, not sticking to a single artist.

1. Describe how you feel today.
2. Describe your best friend.
3. How many times have you been rejected?
4. Tell us the story of your life.

5. How do you act when you are around somebody you like?
6. What did you do today?
7. What has been the craziest thing you have ever done?
8. Describe your favorite concert.
9. Describe how you react when you hear your favorite song on the radio.
10. How many siblings do you have?
11. Complete the sentence: "I am addicted to..."
12. Complete the sentence: "My favorite singer makes me..."
13. How many people have you kissed in your life?
14. How do you feel about drugs?
15. Complete the sentence: "I constantly..."
16. Complete the sentence: "I am..."
17. When people wake you up in the middle of the night, what do you do?
18. Describe your favorite movie.

THE MINI BOYFRIEND TAG: This is not a tag for tiny boy-friends; it is just a shorter version of the main "Boyfriend Tag"! Do this tag interview style, with you asking your boyfriend the questions.

1. Where did we meet?
2. What was our first date?
3. Where was our first kiss, and how was it?
4. When did you know I was the one for you?
5. What was your first impression of me?
6. When did you meet my family?
7. Do we have any traditions as a couple?
8. What was our first road trip together?
9. Who said, "I love you" first, and where were we at?
10. What do we argue about the most?

11. Do you know any of each other's exes?
12. What is your job?
13. Who wears the pants in our relationship?

THE MOM TAG: This is like the "Dad Tag" that appeared earlier in this chapter, except for this one, you are to interview your mom on camera!

1. What was I like as a child?
2. What do you think of my making YouTube videos?
3. What is something funny I did when I was younger?
4. Have you learned anything from me in relation to the content I create for YouTube?
5. What is a weird habit of mine?
6. If you had to rename me, what would my name be?
7. When we go out to eat, what do I order?
8. What is the one thing you wish I would do?
9. What is something I do that annoys you?
10. What is something I obsess over?
11. Where would you like to see me in 10 years?
12. When were you the proudest of me?
13. What is the worst thing I have ever done?
14. What is your favorite moment of us together?
15. How was I in school?
16. What would you change if you could raise me again?
17. Describe my perfect mate?

MUSIC TAG #1: I think there are just as many music-related tags as there are beauty-themed ones! Here is yet another one where you can share your love of music with your viewers.

1. Favorite music genre?
2. Favorite album you own a hard copy of (not digital)?

3. Do you subscribe to any music magazines?
4. Do you own any concert clothing?
5. What is your dream concert to attend?
6. What is your guilty pleasure song?
7. From what artist do you own the most albums?
8. In your digital playlist, from what artist do you have the most songs downloaded?
9. Last song you listen to?
10. How many songs do you have on your phone/MP3 player?
11. Your favorite solo artist?
12. Your favorite band?
13. Least favorite musical genre?
14. First song you ever downloaded?
15. Can you plan any instruments?
16. One artist you want to meet in person?
17. An old artist or band you would like to see make a comeback?
18. What are your top 5 favorite albums you own?
19. What is your all-time favorite music video?

MUSIC TAG #2: Yup, another music tag! As you will see in this tag and other similar ones, often the questions repeat themselves. It is good to choose only one tag to film (or if you do all of them to space them out a bit), or pull the best questions from each of them to create your own unique version!

1. Favorite band/musician of the moment?
2. One band you always come back to?
3. Favorite movie soundtrack?
4. What is/are your favorite song(s) of all time?
5. Most embarrassing song on your iTunes?
6. Top 3 played songs on your iTunes?
7. Favorite concert you have attended?

8. Most underrated musician, in your opinion?
9. Favorite quote or song lyric?

MUST TAG #3: While this is yet another music tag, it does have more original questions than the others in this book!

1. The Beatles or The Stones?
2. Pink Floyd or Led Zeppelin?
3. First album you ever bought?
4. Favorite album of all time?
5. Do you play any instruments? In your mind, when playing your instrument, do you pretend to be anyone?
6. On a scale of 1-10, how cool do you think Iggy Pop is, or was?
7. If you had to be a groupie/roadie of any band, who would it be?
8. When did you last air-guitar?
9. When did you last dance on your own like an idiot?
10. On a scale of 1-10, how good of a dancer are you?
11. Best concert you have ever been to?
12. Do you share any musical tastes with your parents?
13. What are your three favorite genres of music?
14. Which decade do you wish you had grown up in so you could have lived through that generation of music?
15. Favorite guilty pleasure music?
16. If you had to choose to only listen to one song forever, what would it be?
17. Do you write music?
18. Do you still buy CD's/albums, or do you download your music?
19. Favorite guitar solo?
20. Which song would you sing karaoke to?

MY FIRST TIME TAG #1: The "first-time" tags are much more innocent than they sound, although their suggestive titles do tend to bring in more viewers!

1. First Tweet?
2. First YouTube video?
3. First person you subscribed to on YouTube?
4. First Facebook profile pic?
5. Do you still talk to your first love?
6. What was your first alcoholic drink?
7. What was your first job?
8. What was your first car?
9. Who was the first person to text you today?
10. Who is the first person you thought of this morning?
11. Who was your first-grade teacher?
12. Where did you go on your first ride on an airplane?
13. Who was your first best friend, and do you still talk?
14. Where was your first sleepover?
15. What was the first thing you did this morning?
16. What was the first concert you ever went to?
17. First broken bone?
18. First piercing?
19. First foreign country you have gone to?
20. First movie you remember seeing?
21. When was your first detention?
22. Who was your first roommate?
23. If you had one wish, what would it be?
24. What was the first sport you were involved in?
25. What is the first thing you do when you get home?
26. When was your first kiss?

MY FIRST TIME TAG #2: This tag has many the same questions as the last one; again, I recommend you choose only one to do or to combine your favorite questions from each into one video!

1. First YouTube video you ever watched?
2. First person you subscribed to on YouTube?
3. Do you still talk to your first love?
4. First kiss?
5. First alcoholic drink?
6. First car?
7. First job?
8. First pet?
9. First celebrity crush?
10. First real boyfriend/girlfriend?
11. Who was the first person to text you today?
12. Who was your first-grade teacher?
13. Where was your first sleepover?
14. What was the first thing you did this morning?
15. First concert you ever went to?
16. First broken bone?
17. First movie you remember seeing?
18. First sport you were involved in?
19. First tweet?
20. First Facebook profile pic?
21. First piercing?

THE 90'S TAG: If you were a child, teen, or young adult in the 1990s, this is a fun tag that will take you back in time!

1. Favorite Disney Channel original movie?
2. Favorite music artist?
3. Favorite Nick Jr. show?
4. Favorite candy as a kid?
5. Favorite game you played as a kid?
6. Favorite McDonald's Happy Meal toy?
7. Favorite book?
8. Favorite clothing store?
9. What would you watch when you got home from

school?
10. Favorite TV show?
11. Favorite toys?
12. Favorite commercials?
13. NSYNC or Backstreet Boys?
14. Weirdest fashion trend?
15. Favorite collectible?
16. Favorite Beanie Baby?
17. How many Tamagotchi's did you go through?
18. Favorite gaming system and video game?

19 QUESTIONS TAG: This is a fun and easy, "get to know me" tag to film for your audience!

1. Where were you born?
2. Were you named after someone?
3. When was the last time you cried?
4. Do you have any kids?
5. If you were another person, would you be friends with you?
6. Do you have any pets?
7. Do you use sarcasm?
8. Would you bungee jump?
9. What is your favorite cereal?
10. What is your eye color?
11. Do you like sad or happy ending in movies?
12. Do you have any brothers or sisters?
13. Do you prefer a computer or television?
14. What is the first thing you notice about a person?
15. What is your favorite smell?
16. What is the furthest you have ever been from home?
17. Do you have any unique talents?
18. Do you have any hobbies?
19. Are you currently in love?

◆ ◆ ◆

9 "WHAT" TAG: This is one of the tags I talked about earlier in this book as initially being part of a 6-10 tag. However, I have broken them up into their own tags for as each is long enough to dedicate a single video to.

1. Your mother's name?
2. What did you do last weekend?
3. What is the most important part of your life?
4. What would you rather be doing right now?
5. What did you last cry over?
6. What always makes you feel better when you are upset?
7. What is the most important thing you look for in a significant other?
8. What are you worried about?
9. What did you have for breakfast?

100 QUESTIONS TAG: This is definitely the longest tag currently being done on YouTube! To keep your video under 20 minutes, try to keep your answers to "yes," "no," or just a few words.

1. Do you sleep with your closet doors open or closed?
2. Do you take the shampoos and conditioner bottles from hotels?
3. Do you sleep with the sheets tucked in or out?
4. Have you ever stolen a street sign?
5. Do you like to use Post-It notes?
6. Do you cut out coupons but never use them?
7. Would you rather be attacked by a big bear or a swarm of bees?
8. Do you have freckles?

9. Do you always smile for pictures?
10. What is your biggest pet peeve?
11. Do you ever count your steps when you walk?
12. Have you ever peed in the woods?
13. Have you ever pooped in the woods?
14. Do you ever dance even if there is no music playing?
15. Do you chew your pens and pencils?
16. How many people have you slept with this week?
17. What size is your bed?
18. What is your favorite song this week?
19. Is it okay for guys to wear pink?
20. Do you still watch cartoons?
21. What is your least favorite movie?
22. Where would you bury hidden treasure if you had some?
23. What do you drink with dinner?
24. What do you dip a chicken nugget in?
25. What is your favorite food?
26. What movie could you watch over and over again?
27. Last person you kissed?
28. Were you ever a boy/girl scout?
29. Would you ever strip or pose nude in a magazine?
30. When was the last time you wrote a letter to someone on paper?
31. Can you change the oil on a car?
32. Ever gotten a speeding ticket?
33. Ever ran out of gas?
34. Favorite kind of sandwich?
35. Best thing to eat for breakfast?
36. What is your usual bedtime?
37. Are you lazy?
38. When you were a kid, what did you dress up as on Halloween?
39. What is your astrological sign?
40. How many languages can you speak?
41. Do you have any magazine subscriptions?

42. Which are better, Legos or Lincoln Logs?
43. Are you stubborn?
44. Who was better, Leno or Letterman?
45. Ever watch soap operas?
46. Are you afraid of heights?
47. Do you sing in the car?
48. Do you sing in the shower?
49. Do you dance in the car?
50. Ever used a gun?
51. Last time you got a portrait taken by a photographer?
52. Do you think musicals are cheesy?
53. Is Christmas stressful?
54. Ever eat a pierogi?
55. Favorite type of fruit pie?
56. Occupations you wanted to be when you were a kid?
57. Do you believe in ghosts?
58. Ever have a Déjà-vu feeling?
59. Take a daily vitamin?
60. Wear slippers?
61. Wear a bathrobe?
62. What do you wear to bed?
63. First concert?
64. Walmart, Target, or Kmart?
65. Nike or Adidas?
66. Cheetos or Fritos?
67. Peanuts or sunflower seeds?
68. Ever hear of the group Tres Bien?
69. Ever take dance lessons?
70. Is there a profession you picture your future spouse doing?
71. Can you curl your tongue?
72. Ever won a spelling bee?
73. Have you ever cried because you were so happy?
74. Own any record albums?
75. Own a record player?

76. Regularly burn incense?
77. Ever been in love?
78. Who would you like to see in concert?
79. What was the last concert you saw?
80. Hot or cold tea?
81. Tea or coffee?
82. Sugar or snickerdoodle cookies?
83. Can you swim?
84. Can you hold your breath without holding your nose?
85. Are you patient?
86. DJ or band at a wedding?
87. Ever won a contest?
88. Have you had any plastic surgery?
89. Which are better, black or green olives?
90. Can you knit or crochet?
91. Best room for a fireplace?
92. Do you want to get married?
93. If you are married already, how long have you been married?
94. Who was your high school crush?
95. Do you cry and throw a fit until you get your own way?
96. Do you have kids?
97. Do you want kids or more kids?
98. What is your favorite color?
99. What is something memorable that happened to you in middle school?
100. Do you miss anyone right now?

ROOMMATE TAG: This is an excellent tag for college students to film together! If you are out of school, you can still film it if your former roommate lives nearby or is visiting!

1. Did you guys know each other before you became roommates?
2. What did you guys initially think of each other the first time you met?
3. How long did it take until you guys became friends?
4. What do you guys usually argue about?
5. What is one thing that really bothers you that your roommate does?
6. Do you guys both have the same passion for makeup?
7. What does your roommate think of you making You-Tube videos?
8. Who spends the most time getting ready in the morning?
9. What was something that you two did not notice about each other until you became roommates?
10. Do you guys sometimes get fed up with each other from seeing each other too often?
11. How do you avoid tension while living together?
12. What is one rule you guys have while living together?
13. How do you deal with sharing a bathroom?
14. Do you make two separate dinners at night?
15. Nationalities?
16. Do you use your roommate's things without asking?
17. What are your favorite things that you like to do with each other?
18. What happens when one person gets sick?
19. Have you thought about having pets or a pet?
20. What is the funniest thing you have ever done together?
21. Has being roommates helped or hurt your friendship?

17 RANDOM QUESTIONS TAG: This is yet another easy-to-film, get-to-know-you tag, although this one does have some original questions that you will not find in other tags!

1. How did you get your YouTube user name?
2. If you could change your first name to anything, what would it be and why?
3. If you could go back in time and give your younger self advice, what would it be?
4. How old were you when you first learned to blow a bubblegum bubble?
5. What did you want to be when you were little?
6. What do you order at Starbucks?
7. What is the hardest you ever laughed?
8. If you could play any musical instrument, what would it be and why?
9. What is your favorite thing to do when you are upset?
10. What is your favorite movie?
11. What is one food you cannot live without?
12. What is your favorite dessert?
13. What is your favorite pizza topping?
14. Would you rather have the superpower to read minds or the power to be invisible?
15. What did you do for your last birthday?
16. If you had one personal "selfish" wish, what would it be, and why?
17. If you were a Pokémon, what would you be called and what would you look like?

THE SCARY TAG: Love horror movies and haunted houses? Then this tag is just for you!

1. What is the scariest experience you have had to date?
2. Have you ever had a scary paranormal experience?
3. Do you know anyone who has been convicted of a violent crime?
4. Do you like scary movies? If so, what is your favorite?

5. Do you like visiting haunted houses for Halloween?
6. Are you afraid of the dark?
7. Does your town have any scary legends?
8. What is your favorite urban legend?
9. Do you frequently have nightmares?
10. What is the scariest nightmare you have ever had?

THE SEVEN DEADLY SINS OF BEAUTY TAG: As I have mentioned several times, the beauty community was one of the first to become famous on YouTube. This is one of the first beauty-related tags to pop up, which means nearly every beauty lover on YouTube has filmed it!

1. GREED: What is your most inexpensive beauty item? What is your most expensive?
2. WRATH: What beauty products do you have a love/hate relationship with?
3. GLUTTONY: What are your most delicious beauty products?
4. SLOTH: What beauty product do you neglect due to laziness?
5. PRIDE: What beauty product gives you the most self-confidence?
6. LUST: What physical attributes do you find most attractive in the opposite sex?
7. ENVY: What beauty/clothing/accessory items would you most like to receive as a gift?

THE SEVEN "WHO" TAG: Here we are at another of the 6-10 tags I have referenced several times already. This tag of seven questions all focus on the people in your life!

1. Who was the last person you saw?

2. Who was the last person you texted?
3. Who was the last person you hung out with?
4. What was the last person to call you?
5. Who did you last hug?
6. Who is the last person who texted you?
7. What was the last person you said "I love you" to?

THE SHOPAHOLIC TAG: Love to shop? Then grab your camera to film this tag and connect with your fellow shopaholics!

1. Would you consider yourself a shopaholic?
2. How would you classify your style?
3. What store can you not leave without buying at least one thing?
4. Where do you find the best deals?
5. What designer are you willing to splurge on?
6. Do you have a "go-to" shopping outfit?
7. What is your guilty clothing pleasure?
8. What is one staple clothing piece you cannot live without?
9. What is a trend you hope never goes out of style?
10. What trend did you love that passed too quickly?
11. Who is your fashion icon?

THE SISTER TAG: This is a fun tag just for sisters! If both of you have a YouTube channel, considering filming two versions of this with you interviewing each other in separate videos. Upload one to each of your channels and then cross-promote them. When doing cross-promotional videos, make sure to release both videos simultaneously and mention AND include the links to the other channel in your description bar.

1. How old are both of you?

2. Describe each other in one word?
3. Do people ever get you mixed up?
4. What is something that annoys you about one another?
5. What is it like being sisters with a YouTuber?
6. Do you ever argue?
7. What is the best thing about one another?
8. Dish the dirt on each other!
9. Favorite inside joke?
10. Favorite memory together?
11. Are you full, half, or stepsisters?
12. Guess each other's favorite singer/band?
13. Who takes longer to get ready?
14. Heels or flats?
15. Pants or dresses?
16. Favorite animal?
17. If your house was burning down and your entire family and pets were sure to be okay, what one item would you save and why?
18. Comedy, horror, or chick-flick movies?
19. Android or iPhone?
20. Favorite movie?
21. What is something weird that you each eat?
22. Do you have any matching clothing?
23. What is each of your favorite TV shows?

SMALL YOUTUBER TAG: Have you just started making YouTube videos? Do you dream of having millions of subscribers one day but feel like you aren't growing fast enough? Don't worry; you are not alone as there are many other small YouTubers out there. This tag not only helps your viewers get to know you, but it can help you connect with other start-up YouTube channels, which can lead to shout-outs and collaborations!

1. What inspired you to start making videos?
2. How long have you been on YouTube, and have you had other channels in the past?
3. Where do you see yourself and your YouTube channel in 5 years?
4. What message are you trying to get across with your videos?
5. Have your friends and family discovered your channel?
6. What does your user name mean?
7. Who is your favorite YouTuber?

6 "WHERE" TAG: Here, we are back to that 6-10 tag that I broke up into individual videos. This one features all location-based questions and is super quick to film!

1. Where does your best friend live?
2. Where did you last go?
3. Where did you last hang out?
4. Where do you or did you go to school?
5. Where is your favorite place to be?
6. Where did you sleep last night?

THE TAN LINES TAG: This tag should be called the "summer tag," but for some reason, it goes by the name "tan lines tag." Regardless of the title, if you love being outside in the warm weather, you will have fun filming this video!

1. A house on the beach or a house near the lake?
2. Favorite summer hairstyle?
3. Do you become easily tanned, or do you get quickly burned?

4. Have you ever got a henna tattoo done?
5. Campfire or late-night swimming?
6. If you could go somewhere during the summer, where would you go?
7. Bikinis or swimsuits?
8. Summer make-up must-have?
9. How many degrees was it on the hottest day until now where you are at?
10. Have you ever had a summer love?
11. Number one thing on your summer bucket list?
12. Long or short hair during the summer?
13. Do you wear make-up if you are going to the pool or beach?
14. Worst summer memory?

TEENAGE GIRL TAG: This tag was originally entitled the "Common White Girl Tag," but I found that so offensive that I changed the title specifically for this book. ALL girls, regardless of skin color, can have fun filming this video!

1. Favorite Starbucks drink?
2. How long does it take you to get ready in the morning?
3. How many selfies do you take daily?
4. How many Instagram followers do you have?
5. Do you ever say "LOL" or "OMG" aloud?
6. Do you wear the same clothing item more than once without washing it?
7. How many Tweets do you have?
8. Instagram, Twitter, or Tumblr?
9. What do you spend most of your time doing?
10. Who are your favorite YouTubers?
11. How often do you do your nails?
12. Are you a shopaholic?
13. How many times have you watched "Mean Girls"?

14. Do you own a lot of clothes?
15. Do you take pictures of your food before eating to share on social media?
16. Do you wear make-up every day?
17. What are your average grades in school?
18. How do you usually style your hair?
19. Do you always look presentable?

10 "HOW" TAG: Here's number ten of the 6-10 tag that I broke up into individual videos. This tag focuses solely on "how" questions!

1. How did you get one of your scars?
2. How did you celebrate your last birthday?
3. How are you feeling at this moment?
4. How did your night go last night?
5. How did you do in high school?
6. How did you get the shirt you are wearing?
7. How often do you see your best friend(s)?
8. How much money did you spend on frivolous things last month?
9. How old do you want to be when you get married (or how old were you if you already married)?
10. How old will you be on your next birthday?

10 LITTLE BEAUTY SECRETS TAG: Another beauty tag – shocker! This one is short and sweet and does contain some unique questions that differ from the other beauty videos.

1. What is the one product that makes you feel like a million dollars?
2. What is your skincare secret?
3. What is your hair care secret?

4. Any workout tips?
5. Which perfume is your secret weapon?
6. Show a clothing item of yours that always turns head.
7. What is your most treasured piece of jewelry?
8. Who is your style crush?
9. Tell us something about you that we do not know!

10 UNDERRATED YOUTUBE GURUS TAG: If you spend lots of time watching YouTube videos, this is an excellent tag to film as it helps you spread the word about your favorite creators and connect with other viewers who enjoy those channels, too!

1. First person that came to mind when you heard the name of the tag?
2. Someone on YouTube that reminds you of yourself?
3. Someone you watch for pure entertainment?
4. Someone with incredible style?
5. Someone with flawless makeup?
6. Someone with perfect hair?
7. Someone with fewer subscribers than you?
8. Someone with more subscribers than you?
9. Someone whose channel you just found?
10. The person with the most potential to grow?

THANKSGIVING TAG: Even though Thanksgiving is an American holiday, lots of people worldwide are starting to incorporate it into their Novembers!

1. What is your favorite Thanksgiving side dish?
2. What is your favorite Thanksgiving dessert?
3. Do you like just the turkey, only the side dishes, or both?
4. What does your ideal Thanksgiving outfit look like?

5. What is your best Thanksgiving memory?
6. How many words can you make of the word "GOB-BLE"?
7. Least favorite Thanksgiving dish?
8. Do you have any quirky Thanksgiving family traditions?
9. Where do you and your family usually celebrate Thanksgiving?
10. What are you most thankful for?

30 QUESTIONS MUSIC TAG: I told you that beauty, and music tags were the most popular, and here we are at another musically focused video! At 30 questions, this one is long, so keep your answers short to ensure your video does not go on for ages (ideally, you want to keep all videos around 15 minutes).

1. The last song you listened to?
2. Last song you purchased?
3. Song you discovered on YouTube?
4. Favorite soundtrack piece?
5. Favorite band?
6. Favorite solo artist?
7. Favorite album?
8. Best live gig or act you want to see live?
9. Guilty pleasure song?
10. Song you used to hate, but now you like?
11. Song you used to love but now cannot stand?
12. Group you wish had never split?
13. Favorite song from a video game?
14. Favorite song from a film?
15. Favorite song from a commercial?
16. Song you grew up with?
17. First song/alum you ever bought?
18. Album you found accidentally and love?

19. Favorite foreign language song?
20. A song from the year you were born?
21. Song from your favorite music genre?
22. Most overrated song?
23. Song you would recommend to everyone?
24. Song that reminds you of a specific event?
25. Song you cannot help but sing along to?
26. Favorite parody song?
27. Favorite slow song?
28. Favorite fast song?
29. Favorite song at the moment?
30. All-time favorite song

THE THROWBACK TAG: This nostalgic tag is fun for all ages to film!

1. What year were you born?
2. Do you have pictures of yourself from when you were younger? If some, show a few on camera.
3. What television shows did you watch growing up?
4. What did you want to be when you grew up, and have you become that, or do you still want to be that?
5. What were your favorite toys to play with as a child?
6. What is your most embarrassing childhood memory?
7. What music did you love to listen to as a child?
8. What were some of the Halloween costumes you wore as a kid?
9. Do you have any special mementos you've to keep since childhood?
10. Did you have any weird habits as a child?
11. What is the scariest thing you remember that happened to you as a child?
12. How is the world different now from the way it was when you were growing up?

◆ ◆ ◆

13 QUESTIONS TAG: Here is another get-to-know-you tag. None of these questions are very serious, so even the most private or shy YouTube creators should have no problem filming this video!

1. What do you order at Starbucks?
2. What is one thing in your closet that you cannot live without?
3. What is one thing that most people probably do not know about you?
4. Name one thing that you want to do before you die?
5. What is one food that you cannot live without?
6. What quote/phrase do you live your life by?
7. What do you like and dislike about the YouTube community?
8. What is your number one most listened to song on iTunes?
9. What kind of style would you define yourself as having?
10. What is your favorite number?
11. What are two of your hobbies?
12. What are two of your pet peeves?
13. What is one of your guilty pleasures?

THIS OR THAT BEAUTY TAG: This is one of the longest beauty tags out there, but the questions are super easy to answer, which also helps keep the video length down to a reasonable level!

1. Blush or bronzer?
2. Lip gloss or lipstick?
3. Eyeliner or mascara?
4. Foundation or concealer?

5. Neutral or color eye shadow?
6. Pressed or loose eye shadows?
7. Brushes or sponges?
8. OPI or China Glaze nail polish?
9. Long or short nails?
10. Acrylic or natural nails?
11. Bright or dark nail polish?
12. Nail art or plain?
13. Perfume or body splash?
14. Lotion or body butter?
15. Body wash or soap?
16. Lush or Bath & Body Works?
17. Jeans or sweat pants?
18. Long or short sleeve shirts?
19. Dresses or skirts?
20. Stripes or plaids?
21. Flip-flops or sandals?
22. Scarves or hats?
23. Studs or dangly earrings?
24. Necklaces or bracelets?
25. Heels or flats?
26. Cowboy boots or riding boots?
27. Jacket or hoodie?
28. Forever 21 or Charlotte Russe?
29. Abercrombie or Hollister?
30. Saks 5th Avenue or Nordstrom?
31. Curly or straight hair?
32. Bun or ponytail?
33. Bobby pins or butterfly clips?
34. Hair spray or gel?
35. Long or short hair?
36. Light or dark hair?
37. Side-swept bangs or full bangs?
38. Hair up or down?
39. Rain or shine?
40. Summer or winter?

41. Fall or spring?
42. Chocolate or vanilla?
43. East coast or West coast?

TMI TAG: This "too much information" tag is actually relatively innocent, and you can omit any questions you don't' feel comfortable asking. This tag is rather long, so keep your answers short to ensure your video comes in around 15 minutes. If you really like to chat, you can always break this up into two different videos.

1. What are you wearing?
2. Ever been in love?
3. Ever had a terrible breakup?
4. How tall are you?
5. How much do you weigh?
6. Any tattoos?
7. Any piercings?
8. Favorite television show?
9. Favorite band?
10. Favorite song?
11. Someone you miss?
12. How old are you?
13. What is your Zodiac sign?
14. Quality you look for in a partner?
15. Favorite quote?
16. Favorite actor?
17. Favorite color?
18. Loud music or soft?
19. Where do you go when you are sad?
20. How long does it take you to shower?
21. How long does it take you to get ready in the morning?
22. Ever been in a physical fight?
23. What is a turn on for you?

24. What is a turn-off?
25. What is the reason you joined YouTube?
26. What are your fears?
27. Last thing that made you cry?
28. Last time you said you loved someone?
29. Meaning behind your YouTube channel name?
30. Last book you read?
31. The book you are currently reading?
32. Last television you watched?
33. Last person you talked to?
34. The relationship between you and the person you last texted?
35. Favorite food?
36. Place you want to visit?
37. Last place you were?
38. Do you have a crush?
39. Last time you kissed someone?
40. Last time you were insulted?
41. Favorite flavor of sweet?
42. What instruments, if any, do you play?
43. Favorite piece of jewelry?
44. Last sport you played?
45. Last song you sang?
46. Last time you hung out with anyone?
47. Who should answer these questions next?

12 CHRISTMAS QUESTIONS TAG: Holiday tags are best filmed at the start of the season. This is a very popular tag that you will see popping up at the beginning of December with the questions being super-fast and easy to answer!

1. Favorite holiday colors?
2. Biggest holiday pet peeve?
3. Do you plan ahead or procrastinate?

4. How old were you when you stopped believing in Santa?
5. Favorite classic holiday song?
6. Favorite modern holiday song?
7. Favorite Christmas tradition?
8. Real or fake tree?
9. When do you put the Christmas tree up and take it down?
10. Favorite holiday cookie/treat?
11. What is at the top of your tree?
12. Do you decorate outside?
13. What did you always wish for but never got?

20 QUESTIONS TAG: Here is another get-to-know-you tag, although note that this one does lean towards girls and beauty.

1. Thing you cannot leave the house without?
2. Favorite brand of makeup?
3. Favorite flowers?
4. Favorite clothing stores?
5. Favorite perfume?
6. Heels or flats?
7. Do you or did you get good grades in school?
8. Favorite colors?
9. Do you drink energy drinks?
10. Do you drink juice?
11. Do you like swimming?
12. Do you eat fries with a fork?
13. What is your favorite moisturizer?
14. Are you or do you want to get married?
15. Do you get mad easily?
16. Are you into ghost hunting?
17. Any phobias?
18. Do you bite your nails?

19. Have you ever had a near-death experience?
20. Do you drink coffee?

20 QUESTIONS ABOUT MUSIC TAG: Another page, another music tag! However, the questions in this one are very straightforward and easy to answer, making it a relatively quick video to film.

1. Which band or artist do you own the most albums by?
2. What was the last song you listened to?
3. What is in your CD player right now?
4. What was the last concert you attended?
5. What was the greatest concert you have ever been to?
6. What is the worst concert you have ever been to?
7. What is the most musically involved you have ever been?
8. What concert are you looking forward to?
9. What is your favorite band shirt?
10. What musician would you like to hang out with for a day?
11. Who is one musician or group you wish would make a comeback?
12. Who is one band or artist you have never seen live but always wanted to?
13. Name four or more flawless albums.
14. How many music-related videos or DVD's do you own?
15. How many concerts have you been to in total?
16. Who have you seen the most live?
17. What is your favorite movie soundtrack?
18. What was your last musical "phase" before you wizened up?
19. What is your "guilty music pleasure" that you hate to admit to liking?

20 QUESTIONS MOMMY TAG: While the teenage set developed many YouTube tags, here is a great tag just for the moms online! Any mommy can answer these questions regardless of how old their child is.

1. Are you a stay-at-home or work-outside-the-home mom?
2. Would you have it any other way?
3. Do you co-sleep?
4. One must-have gear for baby?
5. How many kids do you plan to have?
6. Do you do date nights with your husband? Is so, how many per month?
7. Your child's favorite TV show?
8. Name one thing you bought before you had your baby but never ended up using?
9. Your child's favorite food?
10. How many cars does your family have?
11. Weight gain before pregnancy, during, after, and now?
12. Dream vacation with your kiddos?
13. Dream vacation without the kiddos?
14. How has your life changed since your baby has been born?
15. Finish the sentence, "It makes my heart melt to see..."
16. Where do you shop for your kids' clothing?
17. Favorite mommy make-up and skincare products?
18. Huggies Diaper Jeans: Yay or Nay?
19. Have you always wanted kids?
20. Best part about being a mom?

21 HAIR QUESTIONS TAG: Finally, a tag that is not about makeup; instead, it is all about hair, ha-ha! Makeup, skincare, and hair styling are all very popular video topics on YouTube, so if beauty is your thing, do not hesitate to jump right in!

1. Why did you start taking better care of your hair?
2. What are your two favorite hair products?
3. Whose hair did you admire as a child?
4. What is your ultimate goal length?
5. How are you going to celebrate when you reach your ultimate goal length?
6. Two styles you want to try at your goal length?
7. Which do you prefer: health or length?
8. Which do you prefer: hair ties with no metal parts or butterfly clips?
9. What products do you prefer: salon brands, organic brands, or drugstore brands?
10. Which product or technique do you think is over-rated?
11. Which product/technique do you think is under-rated?
12. What is your favorite part of your hair regimen?
13. What is the most annoying part of your hair regimen?
14. Oils or Butters?
15. Buns or Ponytails?
16. Wigs or Weaves?
17. What is your opinion of growth aids?
18. At what length do you consider hair long?
19. When is the last time you visited a salon?
20. What types of hair information do you pursue most often online: YouTube videos, blogs, or discussion forums?
21. And finally, what piece of advice would you give to someone just starting out on their hair journey?

22 LIFE QUESTIONS TAG: This tag offers lots of thought-provoking questions, but be careful about rambling on or else your video will quickly balloon to an hour-long! YouTube really prefers videos that are 10-15 minutes in length, so keep that in mind when filming and editing.

1. How old would you be if you did not know how old you are?
2. If life is so short, why do we do so many things we don't' like and like so many things we don't do?
3. What is the one thing you would most like to change about the world?
4. If the average human life span was 40 years, how would you live your life differently?
5. Are you more worried about doing things right or doing the right things?
6. If you could offer a newborn child only one piece of advice, what would it be?
7. Would you break the law to save a loved one?
8. What is something you know you do differently than most people?
9. What one thing have you not done that you really want to do? What is holding you back?
10. Are you holding onto something you need to let go of?
11. If you had to move to a state or country besides the one you currently live in, where would it be and why?
12. Which is worst, when a good friend moves away or losing touch with a good friend who lives right by you?
13. What are you most grateful for?
14. Would you rather lose all your old memories or never be able to make new ones?
15. Has your greatest fear ever come true?
16. Do you remember that time five years ago when you were extremely upset? Does it really matter now?
17. What is your happiest childhood memory?
18. Have you ever been with someone, said nothing, and walked away feeling like you just had the best conversation ever?
19. If you just won a million dollars, would you quit your

job?

20. What is the difference between being alive and truly living?
21. What would you do differently if you knew nobody would judge you?
22. Decisions are being made right now. The question is: are you making them for yourself, or are you letting others make them for you?

THE TWILIGHT SAGA TAG: Bella and Edward...or Bella and Jacob? If you have a strong opinion about the "Twilight" books and movies, this is the tag for you!

1. Which book in the series is your favorite?
2. How long did it take you to read the books?
3. Who introduced you to the books?
4. What is your dream ending to the series?
5. Who is your favorite vampire?
6. Who is your favorite werewolf?
7. What one of your favorite quotes from the books?
8. What was your favorite Bella/Edward moment?
9. What was your favorite Bella/Jacob moment?
10. Which book cover was your favorite?
11. Who do you want to see Bella with most, Edward or Jacob?
12. Have you watched all the movies?
13. Did you see the movies in the theatre or on video?
14. Do you own all the movies on DVD or Blu-ray?
15. Who were your favorite actors in the movies?
16. Which actors did you not like?
17. In which book did you like Bella best?
18. In which book did you like Edward best?
19. In which book did you like Jacob best?
20. Which actor would you most like to meet?

THE TWIN TAG: Use your twin power to film this fun tag video! If you both have YouTube channels, each of you can film a video interviewing the other one and then cross-promote the videos on each other's channels!

1. Who is the oldest?
2. Can you show an old photo of the two of you together?
3. Favorite memory together?
4. Each other's dream jobs?
5. Who takes longer to get ready in the morning?
6. Do you have anything matching?
7. Did you ever dress alike?
8. Song you would describe each other?
9. What color are your auras?
10. One thing that you can do well that others cannot?
11. Do you have the same personalities?
12. Silliest question about being twins?
13. Describe each other in one word?
14. One thing that annoys you about each other?
15. If you could go anywhere in the world together, where would it be and why?
16. Nicknames you have for each other
17. What do you order at fast-food restaurants?
18. Favorite thing about each other?
19. Favorite inside joke?
20. Are you identical or fraternal twins?

WINTERLICIOUS TAG: Here is the final seasonal tag in this book, and once again, some of the questions are beauty-related. However, feel free to omit any questions that do not apply to you and/or add any others you think up!

1. Favorite winter nail polish?
2. Favorite winter lip product?
3. Most worn winter clothing piece?
4. Most worn winter accessory?
5. Favorite winter scent or candle?
6. Favorite winter beverage?
7. All-time favorite Christmas or holiday movie?
8. Favorite holiday song?
9. Favorite holiday food or treat?
10. What is your favorite Christmas decoration this year?
11. What is at the top of your wish list?
12. What are your plans for the holidays this year?

THE WOULD YOU RATHER BEAUTY TAG #1: This is the first of TWO would-you-rather beauty tags. I suggest either filming both but spacing them out OUR combining your favorite questions from each into one video.

1. Would you rather go out with messy hair and nice make-up OR nice hair and no make-up?
2. Would you rather shave your eyebrows OR have your eyelashes fall out?
3. Would you rather be forced to shop at only MAC OR Sephora for the rest of your life?
4. Would you rather wear lip gloss and lip liner OR an 80's perm?
5. Would you rather leave the house with an obvious foundation line OR an overdone blush?
6. Would you rather wear MC Hammer pants OR biker shorts in public?
7. Would you rather have a bad orange spray tan OR really weird tan lines that cannot be covered?
8. Would you rather have a bad haircut OR a bad hair color?

9. Would you rather have YouTube OR Twitter taken away forever?
10. Would you rather give up using makeup brushes OR mascara?

❖ ❖ ❖

THE WOULD YOU RATHER BEAUTY TAG #2: Finally, the very last beauty tag in this book! This one is an extension of the one before; as I said, you can film each separately or edit the questions to combine them into a single video.

1. Would you rather walk around all day with your skirt tucked into your underwear OR be seen wearing a really see-through dress?
2. Would you rather go to a party and not realize until the end of the night that you have lipstick on your teeth OR that your fake lashes were coming unglued?
3. Would you rather forget to put mascara on one eye OR forget blush on one side of your face?
4. Would you rather wear a lipstick and lip liner combo OR frosty blue eye shadow?
5. Would you rather wear foundation that is two shades too light OR go way overboard on bronzer?
6. Would you rather drink an entire bottle of ketchup OR run into the guy who broke your heart on a bad hair day with your skin breaking out?
7. Would you rather be able to date any celebrity you wanted OR wake up with perfect red-carpet-worthy hair?
8. Would you rather your armpits smell musky or like delicious lasagna?
9. Would you rather give up your make-up OR your cell phone for one year?
10. Would you rather run into a cute guy you like with food stuck in your teeth OR wearing no make-up at all?

◆ ◆ ◆

THE WOULD YOU RATHER TAG: This is a very long tag with questions that lead to long answers. My suggestion is either to pick out your favorite questions or break this one up into two separate videos.

1. Would you rather live in a world where you rule OR live in a world with no problems?
2. Would you rather always take a cold shower OR sleep an hour less than you need to be fully rested?
3. Would you rather always have to say everything on your mind OR never speak again?
4. Would you rather lose OR never play?
5. Would you rather always wear earmuffs OR a nose plug?
6. Would you rather be 3-feet tall OR 8-feet tall?
7. Would you rather be a dog named Killer OR a cat named Fluffy?
8. Would you rather be a giant hamster OR a tiny rhino?
9. Would you rather be able to hear any conversation OR take back anything you say?
10. Would you rather be able to read everyone's mind all of the time OR always know their future?
11. Would you rather be able to stop time OR fly?
12. Would you rather be born with an elephant truck OR a giraffe neck?
13. Would you rather be forced to tell your best friend a lie OR your parents the truth?
14. Would you rather be forgotten OR hatefully remembered?
15. Would you rather go about your typical day naked OR fall asleep for a year?
16. Would you rather be gossiped about OR never talked about at all?

17. Would you rather be hairy all over OR entirely bald?
18. Would you rather be happy for 8 hours a day and poor OR sad for 8 hours a day and rich?
19. Would you rather be invisible OR be able to read minds?
20. Would you rather be rich and ugly OR poor and good looking?
21. Would you rather be stranded on an island alone OR with someone you hate?
22. Would you rather be the most popular OR the smartest person you know?
23. Would you rather eat a bar of soap OR drink a bottle of dishwashing liquid?
24. Would you rather eat a handful of hair OR lick three public telephones?
25. Would you rather eat a tub of BUTTER OR a gallon of ice cream?
26. Would you rather eat a tub of margarine OR 5 tablespoons of hot pepper sauce?
27. Would you rather eat poison ivy OR a handful of bumblebees?
28. Would you rather end hunger OR hatred?
29. Would you rather find true love OR 10 million dollars?
30. Would you rather forget who you were OR who everyone else was?
31. Would you rather give bad advice OR take bad advice?
32. Would you rather give up your computer OR your pet?
33. Would you rather go to an amusement park OR a family reunion?
34. Would you rather go without television OR junk food for the rest of your life?
35. Would you rather have a beautiful house and an ugly car OR an ugly house and a gorgeous car?

36. Would you rather have a kangaroo OR koala as your pet?
37. Would you rather have a missing finger OR have an extra toe?
38. Would you rather have one wish granted today OR three wishes granted in 10 years?
39. Would you rather have x-ray vision OR bionic hearing?
40. Would you rather kiss a jellyfish OR step on a crab?
41. Would you rather know it all OR have it all?
42. Would you rather live without music OR television?
43. Would you rather love but not be loved back OR be loved but never love in return?
44. Would you rather never use the internet again OR never watch television again/
45. Would you rather only be able to whisper OR only be able to shout?
46. Would you rather own a ski lodge OR a surf camp?
47. Would you rather publish your diary OR make a movie about your most embarrassing moment?
48. Would you rather spend all day surfing the internet OR the ocean?

ZOMBIE APOCALYPSE TAG: It is somewhat appropriate that the final tag on this list relates to the potential end of the world!

1. Which three YouTubers would you have in your team?
2. The object immediately to your left is your only weapon – what is it?
3. If you were a zombie, who would you want to bite?
4. What would your survival plan be?
5. What would you do if your parents became zombies?
6. Do you want the zombie apocalypse to happen?

CONCLUSION

With just a camera and a computer, anyone can start a YouTube channel. However, it takes commitment and perseverance to make MONEY on the site. While there are a handful of people who have gotten rich over the years by making videos, for most people, YouTube offers a bit of extra spending money, perhaps even enough to qualify it as a part-time job. How much you earn is up to you in regards to how much time and effort you are willing to put into producing quality content that viewers respond to.

Putting yourself out there in front of thousands and potentially millions of people is a scary proposition. However, if you approach YouTube for your own personal enjoyment and growth before anything else, you will have a successful channel that also brings you some income.

With all the work involved, why do I make YouTube videos? Because it is FUN! I love connecting with other resellers through my Ebay videos on my *The Reselling Report with Ann Eckhart* channel. I also love to share lifestyle content on my *Ann Eckhart Vlogs* channel. However, not only do I enjoy creating my videos, but they also earn my money through AdSense and sponsorships plus affiliate and referral links. My videos also drive traffic to my Amazon Author Page, where I sell my books. Sometimes viewers buy the merchandise I have for sale, both from the TeeSpring links that appear under my videos and my TeePublic store, which I link in my description box.

My YouTube channel works in coordination with my blog and social media sites to help solidify my brand. My YouTube channels drive traffic to my other sites, and my other sites drive traffic to my YouTube channels. All work together to create the businesses that I run from the comfort of my own home with only myself to answer to. I love being my own boss and working from home!

I am on YouTube for fun AND profit! Hopefully, the tips in this book will give you the confidence to begin your own YouTube journey. As the saying goes: Do what you love, and the money will follow. Have FUN on YouTube and watch your PROFIT add up!

ABOUT THE AUTHOR

Ann Eckhart is an author, YouTube creator, and reseller based in Iowa. She has written numerous books about selling on Ebay as well as making money on YouTube. She also designs planners, journals, and notebooks under the Jean Lee Publishing pen name. Check out her Amazon Storefront at https://amzn.to/3551WR2 for all her titles.

You can keep up with everything Ann does on her blog at www.AnnEckhart.com. You can also connect with her on the following social media networks:

FACEBOOK: https://www.facebook.com/anneckhart/

TWITTER: https://twitter.com/ann_eckhart

INSTAGRAM: https://www.instagram.com/ann_eckhart/

THE RESELLING REPORT YOUTUBE CHANNEL: https://tinyurl.com/y4tb92dy

ANN ECKHART VLOGS YOUTUBE CHANNEL: https://tinyurl.com/yxjqn6d2

If you enjoyed this book, please be sure to leave it a 5-star review on Amazon: https://amzn.to/2B99zFL

COPYRIGHT 2020